I0815144

THE AMERICAN REVOLUTION ON TRIAL

THE REVOLUTIONARY AGE

Francis D. Cogliano, Christa Breault Dierksheide,
Eliga H. Gould, and Patrick Griffin, Editors

The American Revolution on Trial

A New Nation Confronts the Burden of Independence

T. H. BREEN

UNIVERSITY OF VIRGINIA PRESS
Charlottesville and London

The University of Virginia Press is situated on the traditional lands of the Monacan Nation, and the Commonwealth of Virginia was and is home to many other Indigenous people. We pay our respect to all of them, past and present. We also honor the enslaved African and African American people who built the University of Virginia, and we recognize their descendants. We commit to fostering voices from these communities through our publications and to deepening our collective understanding of their histories and contributions.

University of Virginia Press

Printed in the United States of America on acid-free paper

First published 2026

9 8 7 6 5 4 3 2 1

ISBN 978-0-8139-5497-4 (hardback)
ISBN 978-0-8139-5499-8 (ebook)

Library of Congress Cataloging-in-Publication Data is available for this title.

Cover art: Soldier, from masthead of the *Independent Chronicle*, Boston, 1781; eagle, by John Cotton Smith (courtesy of Compositor database)
Cover design: Cecilia Sorochin

Per Susan che ha condiviso l'intero viaggio

• CONTENTS •

• INTRODUCTION •

On Prospect Hill

My acquaintance with Colonel David Henley owes a great deal to luck. Many years ago, I was going through catalogues distributed by rare and antique book stores. To be sure, this quirky interest may not be to everyone's taste, but for me, there was always a chance of finding surprising and affordable bargains. One general listing focused on books and maps published in the late eighteenth century. Moreover, many of these items were associated with the American Revolution, and although the most tempting entries were well out of my price range, one title immediately caught my attention.

The dealer provided a dauntingly wordy title: *Proceedings of a Court-Martial, Held at Cambridge, By Order of Major General Heath, Commanding the American Troops for the Northern District, for the Trial of Colonel David Henley, accused by General Burgoyne of Ill Treatment of British Soldiers.* It had been published in London in 1778, in other words, during the War for Independence. More out of curiosity than as part of a long-term plan, I purchased it.

At the time I knew nothing about the Henley trial. The title alone, however, begged obvious questions. Burgoyne was a celebrated, some would say, infamous figure associated forever with the surrender in 1777 of a large British army at Saratoga, New York.

What circumstances, I wondered, could possibly explain why an English general of his social standing—but now a prisoner of war—would accuse an American officer of a crime? A quick reading of the *Proceedings* provided hints about the strange proceeding in a courtroom in Cambridge, Massachusetts, more than a year after the signing of the Declaration of Independence. It contained detailed interrogations of ordinary soldiers—American and British—as well as technical legal appeals by the prosecutor and by the attorney who mounted an inspired defense of Colonel Henley. However, the mysterious circumstances surrounding the event lacked explanation.

Although closer examination of the text brought rewards, the court records sparked new puzzles. They suggested a much more complex narrative than I had originally anticipated. To be sure, the controversy at Cambridge involved dramatic personal confrontations—inflated egos, intrigue and subterfuge, fear and misinformation. To my surprise, it also suggested a perspective on the American Revolution that had long been hiding in plain sight.

In fact, the trial opened a window onto how Americans who were not famous founding fathers tried to make sense of the revolutionary experiences that radically changed their society. What was at stake in the Cambridge courtroom was not simply the question of an American colonel's guilt or innocence—a matter never fully resolved—but more significantly, it revealed a troubling uncertainty, even after a formal declaration of independence, about the honor and reputation of the United States in a world of allegedly more civilized nations.

Quite unexpectedly, the trial served as a reminder that even during the war, revolutionary Americans remained defensive about how they—as representatives of a new republic—should behave. Were they somehow still British despite their fight for independence? Throughout the trial, Burgoyne cleverly mocked their cultural insecurities, forcing them to confront the full implications of independence. Were they capable of maintaining a rule of law? Was the young republic worthy of the respect of other countries? Could Americans deliver justice to an enemy general they thoroughly disliked?

The trial centered on several strong-willed men whose lives were shaped by the Revolution. The fortunes of William Heath, David Henley, William Tudor, and John Burgoyne became intertwined multiple times over several years. They were repeatedly forced to evaluate each other's motives and character, strengths and weaknesses, all within the context of developing a fuller understanding of the challenge of independence. The ties binding them were initially forged during the immediate aftermath of the Battle of Bunker Hill. After that moment, the vicissitudes of war brought them together again during the long, winter march of British and German prisoners to Cambridge after Burgoyne surrendered at Saratoga in 1777. Then, by chance, the characters in this revolutionary drama clashed openly in a prison camp and later in a small courtroom.

The issues raised in that courtroom could not be contained. In the midst of a conflict going badly, the Continental Congress, which was then trying to escape capture by the British, felt compelled to spend precious time debating how best to treat Burgoyne, who was a prisoner of war. With the very survival of the nation at stake, the nation's representatives debated how a truly civilized country should behave in the world of nations. The same questions raised at a trial in Cambridge perplexed the legislators. Did the United States stand for the rule of law? Was it an honorable nation? Did it merit the respect of other countries, even when that country was Great Britain?

That the founding generation of the United States cared so deeply about establishing its national and international reputation for justice is not simply a matter of historical concern. It involves more than a better understanding of how Americans experienced the Revolution. The topic resonates in our own political culture. For that reason, the story of the continuing burden of independence draws us back to a winter afternoon on Prospect Hill.

• CHAPTER 1 •

Soft Colonialism

The story of our nation's founding recounted here challenges much that Americans take for granted about their Revolution.[1] It explores how ordinary people experienced major political and cultural change in their lives, and in the process gave personal meaning to the Revolution itself. A new narrative of the founding period begins not with the fight at Lexington and Concord or the signing of the Declaration of Independence, but with a disturbance in a prisoner-of-war camp on a cold December afternoon. That seemingly minor event put the American Revolution on trial. At the moment that George Washington was barely holding the army together, a scuffle between an American colonel and a British prisoner of war on Prospect Hill, which was then located in Charlestown, Massachusetts, sparked a far-reaching review of the meaning of independence for citizens and soldiers who had just created a new republic.

The explanation for this ordeal requires setting aside time-honored accounts of the Revolution—tales of gifted leaders and military victories. There is a welcome payoff for revising an oft-told-story. By shifting the focus away from familiar histories of nationhood, we can better understand how Americans in the midst of war actually construed independence.[2] The revolutionary adjustment to a new political environment was difficult, tentative, and problematic. It was in this uncertain situation that a confrontation between an American guard and British prisoner triggered an impassioned debate about national honor. At stake was whether an independent United States was worthy of the respect of other sovereign nations throughout the world, including, most unexpectedly in the midst of revolution, Great Britain.

* * *

Histories of the American Revolution generally concentrate on the actions of gifted and heroic founders. Whatever the merits of this approach, we might ask how these tumultuous events played out in places far from the battlefield or legislative centers. The people of Massachusetts faced such a challenge during the winter of 1777–78. The prerevolutionary riots over parliamentary taxes and British occupation of Boston were memories, painful to be sure, but the war had moved away. And then, quite unexpectedly, it returned, not as immediate military peril but rather with the sudden creation of a huge prisoner-of-war camp for an army of approximately six thousand British and German troops who had just surrendered at Saratoga on October 17, 1777. Under the command of Major General John Burgoyne, these troublesome arrivals forced Americans who simply wanted to restore the routines of everyday life to confront the challenge of independence.

The incident precipitating this crisis—one that put the American Revolution on trial—involved a young, highly respected Continental officer who may or may not have employed excessive force to subdue an obstreperous British prisoner. The charges against him were never fully resolved. Whatever the truth, Colonel David Henley's actions at that decisive moment launched one of the more bizarre courts-martial in American history. The central legal question, of course, was Henley's possible guilt—in other words, according to the military code of justice, had he performed under stress as an officer and gentleman?

Henley's defense quickly merged with a much larger revolutionary story. The entire episode compelled everyone involved—military authorities as well as ordinary citizens—to consider issues that had not been adequately addressed during the early days of conflict with Great Britain. The list includes what it meant to be an American. After declaring their independence, they wondered, were the revolutionaries in some fundamental respect still English? There was no single answer. It took many decades before Americans voiced what we would recognize as full-throated nationalism. The process of forging a cultural identity that was not British began much earlier, in fact, while victory was still in doubt. Henley's trial was a dramatic case of this larger issue. His ordeal revealed how inchoate notions about independence crystalized within a local and personal context. It was here that abstract revolutionary principles acquired emotional charge. To be sure, Americans had previously rejected monarchy and declared the birth of a new republic. What remained to be settled during the trial was how much former colonists remained tied to the culture of Great Britain.[3]

The entire controversy was bizarre. The proceedings certainly did not follow normal expectations.[4] The person who accused Henley of a serious crime was none other than Burgoyne, who became a prisoner of war after his defeat at Saratoga. He insisted that the American officers to whom he had just surrendered bring Henley to a general court-martial. The demand had no precedent in American military law. Even under the British system this was a highly questionable request. Despite that fact, Major General William Heath, the senior Continental officer in New England, acquiesced repeatedly to Burgoyne's demands. To Heath's surprise, however, authorizing a full court-martial failed to dampen Burgoyne's audacity. The British general also announced his intention to serve as a prosecutor during the trial with the right to interrogate witnesses—British and American. Since Heath had already appointed an American judge advocate for that purpose, there seemed no justification for Burgoyne's participation. But, again, quite unexpectedly, Heath gave way.

To place this unusual story in broader historical perspective, one must imagine General Robert E. Lee trying to persuade the United States Army to court-martial one of Ulysses Grant's trusted lieutenants. Or, at the end of World War II, learning that General Dwight Eisenhower had allowed a German officer to bring charges of misconduct against an American soldier. Such requests would have been summarily dismissed. And yet with the outcome of the Revolutionary War in doubt—the Continental Army was barely holding out at Valley Forge—Heath offered only mild objections to Burgoyne's requests.[5]

What, we wonder, could possibly explain Heath's astonishing decisions? What gave the defeated Burgoyne such bargaining power? The answer to these questions lies in transcripts of the Henley trial and a rich correspondence among the various participants. This clash of personalities—a proud New England farmer and a self-important English aristocrat, an honored Continental officer and a rising legal star—invites a new perspective on the American Revolution.

* * *

General Heath's extraordinary reaction to Burgoyne's demands remains a puzzle so long as we interpret the ordeal within a traditional narrative of the Revolution. The textbook story about American independence usually depicts the colonists as children who at some critical moment exclaimed that they were mature enough to handle their own political affairs. What propelled them to final separation from Great Britain were a series of parliamentary taxes—the Stamp Act (1765) and the Tea Act (1773), for example. We learn that American discontent built slowly, primarily in the major ports, but as it gradually became clear that George III and his ministers had no intention of accommodating colonial arguments against taxation without representation, an aggrieved people turned reluctantly to armed resistance. The account that Americans absorb in school begins with the coronation of George III (1761) and concludes triumphantly with Thomas Paine's *Common Sense* (1776) and the Declaration of Independence.[6] Some versions even commence with the original seventeenth-century colonization of New England or Virginia on the assumption that once the first settlers breathed the free air of the New World, it was only a matter of time before they separated from a distant regime.

The problem with this long-established chronicle of the breakdown of British rule over the mainland colonies is not that it is wrong. Rather, the issue is that this story of the Revolution overlooks other developments shaping American perceptions of independence. The popular version of the Revolution focuses almost exclusively on the erosion of political ties—on contested perceptions of the British constitution, colonial charters, American petitions, and parliamentary statutes.[7]

From this starting point, it follows logically that accounts of the collapse of imperial power will inevitably concentrate on the actions of the men who actually wielded power, be they a small group of American founding fathers who drafted lawyerly arguments against taxation without representation or a number of British leaders usually depicted as pigheaded or grossly ignorant or both. The parade of notable figures includes Thomas Jefferson, John Adams, and John Dickinson, and on the British side, George Grenville, Earl of Bute, and Lord North. Lesser-known people go missing, since in a history of celebrated political leaders, they are usually treated as spectators of their own revolution.

Drawing attention to the confusion between political and cultural independence is fundamental to our story. Of course, it would involve a gross misrepresentation of our history to claim that declaring independence from Great Britain was an effortless move. The risk of failure was very great. It precipitated a difficult war lasting eight years. For most revolutionaries the decision to fight for independence involved public commitment. There was seldom a safe middle ground. Committees of safety and observation identified enemies to the cause. Punishments for giving aid and comfort to the British were severe. Political compromise proved a nonstarter after the Battles of Lexington and Concord. At the time, no one put forward the idea that the colonies could assume a commonwealth status as did Canada many years later. Although Americans were not quite sure on July 4, 1776, how a stable republican government might be organized, the signers of the Declaration were prepared to take a chance on separation.

Achieving cultural independence from the mother country was an entirely different matter.[8] It was especially difficult for Americans who had grown accustomed to a bundle of quotidian assumptions about how to act and what to believe within an imperial world. By 1776, they largely took these unwritten rules of behavior for granted. Tradition weighed heavily on revolutionaries. For that reason, a cultural adjustment after separation from Great Britain was much slower, although no less difficult than the political one. It involved not only normative expectations about the use and possession of the objects of material culture but also reflexive notions about social interaction acquired from long personal experience. The key point is that, from this perspective, defining independence was a process, a fluid, ongoing act of self-discovery as people filled a largely empty category—independence—with personal meaning.

The story is certainly not uniquely American. After all, as many twentieth-century examples reveal, refashioning cultural identity is a challenge that colonized peoples throughout the world regularly confront at the moment of independence from an imperial state. Since the end of World War II, we have witnessed cases of cultural decoupling from a self-proclaimed mother country as a postcolonial phenomenon. There is a lesson in this experience for us. It suggests that much of the history of the American Revolution is more aptly compared with the decolonization of Algeria, Nigeria, or India than with the French or Russian Revolutions.[9]

Comparisons of this sort are instructive. Crises involving cultural identity reveal that while the people living in recently liberated colonies enthusiastically celebrate political independence, they are often uncertain about how established nations will perceive them. To be sure, they welcome separation, but that accomplishment seldom alleviates an apprehension that they might not measure up to the expectations of their former rulers. This edginess reflects a suspicion that even after waging successful armed rebellion, they may not in fact be as civilized as the men and women who once set the standard for enlightened beliefs and behavior. They are uncertain, often defensive. Did political independence, they wonder, somehow lessen them in some fundamental way? Have they, in fact, managed to sustain a genuine rule of law?

Former colonial societies that have wrestled with these challenges sometimes give in to the temptation to have their cake and eat it too; in other words, to enjoy political independence while at the same time preserving aspects of an older imperial culture. After all, it is never easy to divorce a set of expectations about a general culture from habit and memory. Even the most rebellious colonial subjects find themselves at the moment of independence tied to a mother country by books published in imperial capitals, law codes established long before political liberation, and fashionable tastes associated with distant centers such as London or Paris. These links are very hard to repudiate, even when one knows they are expressions of an imperial regime. In this situation, giving up a popular style of dress or an imported wine can be as difficult as renouncing a king.

Although the story of the American Revolution we like to tell ourselves seldom involves postcolonial experience, the relevance of a comparative framework for our own history is undeniable. Recent scholarship on the character of colonial society before independence indicates that during the eighteenth century white Americans were becoming more, not less, British with each passing decade.[10] (The focus here is on white colonists, since the large percentage of the population that was African American and enslaved were struggling to preserve their own cultural traditions and independence.)[11] The popular notion that European colonists were like children who were gradually distancing themselves from the mother country cannot stand up to critical examination. The growing eighteenth-century identification with England and all things English is called Anglicization, an awkward term to be sure, but one that reflects what was actually happening in the thirteen mainland colonies. The revolutionary mentality was shaped as much by nostalgia as by a desire to remake the world.

The appeal of an imagined distant homeland drew strength from the conviction that the British constitution was the best guarantee of personal liberty that had ever existed. Added to that belief was a happy assurance that the British Empire would defend Protestantism against Catholicism.[12] It is no surprise that the colonists feared and despised the French in Canada. And when king and Parliament asked the Americans to support a war against France—the Seven Years' War (1756–63)—the colonists strove to demonstrate unquestioned loyalty to the British Empire. On the basis of their contribution, they fancied that they were equal partners in the imperial contest.[13] At the moment of victory, for example, one American newspaper confidently declared that, as a result of the conquest of Canada (1763), "the spirited *Englishman,* the mountainous *Welshman,* the brave *Scotchman,* and *Irishman,* and the loyal *American,* may be firmly united and mutually be happily restored, Civil War disappointed, and each agree to embrace, as *British Brothers,* in defending the Common Cause."[14]

The ambitions of most colonists from ancient Rome to modern times have been held in check by coercion. The soldiers of empire have maintained order. But that was most emphatically not the case with the American colonies. Imperial loyalty depended not on raw force but on the appealing embrace of commerce. As English manufacturing expanded rapidly during the eighteenth century, the colonies offered a huge marketplace for various exported goods. Other European powers were prohibited from trading in American ports. With rare exception, English rulers saw no reason to interfere with this mutually beneficial relationship. American products such as tobacco flowed to English and Scottish ports; British ships supplied the colonists with the manufactured objects they desired.[15]

The policy governing this lightly regulated system was known as "salutary neglect," a relatively nonintrusive commercial system enriching English merchants and bringing a higher standard of living to the Americans, even those aggressively populating the frontier.[16] A better description for this system would be *soft colonialism,* a form of imperial control founded on the exchange of goods. Adam Smith praised the relationship, but, perhaps not surprisingly, many contemporaries defended tighter authority. Benjamin Franklin also understood the character of this system, informing the House of Commons in 1766 that British rule in America never depended on "forts, citadels, garrisons or armies." He reminded the members of Parliament that the Americans "were governed by this country [England] at the expense only of a little pen, ink and paper. They were led by a thread."[17]

Striking evidence for this happy thread of authority could be found in any colonial newspaper. Weekly journals published valuable information about the arrival of British ships bearing a wide range of goods. Stores advertised alluring inventories; merchants enticed customers with offers of easy credit. The notion that colonial Americans were self-sufficient—or even wanted to be—has no validity. Entire families, including women and children, worked on farms to obtain enough money to purchase metal goods and glassware from tradesmen.[18] The rapid expansion of slavery was an odious response to this rising consumer demand. Textiles were far and away the major imported item. English weavers produced huge amounts of woolen cloth as well as lighter linen and cotton fabric. Colonists soon discovered it was much easier to purchase the cloth for garments at local shops than to struggle long hours with inadequate spinning wheels.

This vibrant eighteenth-century marketplace not only offered choice and convenience but also allowed ordinary people to indulge in self-fashioning. For the first time, they could select colors and patterns. Like modern consumers, colonists demanded up-to-date styles. One visitor to a colonial town was surprised to find that "the quick importation of fashions from the mother country is adopted earlier by the polished and affluent American than by many opulent persons in the great metropolis [London]." The report may have exaggerated the vivacity of the colonial market—but not by much. He later noted, "At present, it is evident that almost every article of use or ornament is to be obtained on much more reasonable terms from the mother country than from artisans settled on this side [of] the Atlantic. It is also certain that goods of every kind produced or manufactured in England are greatly superior to the produce or manufactures on this continent."[19]

The practical implications of soft colonialism have not been explored. The run-up to actual independence provides an instructive example. The bitter controversies of the 1760s and 1770s over taxation without representation strained the loose political ties that had long governed the empire. But even as American petitions and appeals turned to violence, the colonists did not welcome severing their cultural bonds with Great Britain. It is true that they organized increasingly effective boycotts of English imported goods, but the weaponizing of the marketplace in no way indicated that the American desire to obtain the manufactured items that they could not produce themselves had diminished. The newspapers still carried the same inventories of consumer desire. Americans read books published in the mother country, attended plays first produced in London, and prayed in churches that owed their existence to religious movements in England. In *Common Sense,* Thomas Paine railed against monarchy, but he had little to say about the soft colonialism holding the empire together by a thread.

Again, we encounter a conflation of political and cultural independence. As Franklin observed after the fighting started, English rulers had foolishly disrupted a system that had worked well for a long time. In a meeting with English negotiators in July 1776, he reported that military aggression had "extinguished every remaining Spark of Affection for the Parent Country we once held so dear." It was a sad moment: "Long did I endeavour with unfeigned and unwearied Zeal to preserve from breaking, that fine and noble China Vase the British Empire: for I knew that being once broke, the separate Parts could not retain even their Share of the Strength that existed in the Whole."[20]

It is a curious aspect of our revolutionary narrative that after Americans finally broke with Great Britain, they did not describe the enemy with the kind of vitriol that one might have expected. As they mounted a military campaign against British troops, they spoke of separation in almost sentimental terms, as if they could not quite understand how friends could come to such a pass. And this is precisely the point. The argument is not that the colonists were not angry with the mother country. They were. Enough to wage war.

The odd element about the Revolution was that when the outcome of the war was still very much in doubt, Americans did not seem to have been as alienated from Great Britain as one might expect. At the moment of declaring independence, there was no equivalent in the American revolutionary story to the storming of the Bastille in Paris, the White and Red Terror of Russia, or the chronic revolts in Haiti. Even after the occupation of Boston and the capture of New York City, Americans who supported independence expressed a longing for a former time when the British Empire had stood for security, prosperity, and liberty. The cultural bonds with the mother country remained strong. This ambivalence about what it actually meant to live with independence—liberated from king and Parliament but still wedded to familiar English beliefs and practices and eager to experience better material conditions—helps explain why comparison with the French and Russian Revolutions seldom generates significant insights about our experience. Stated bluntly, revolutionary Americans accustomed to the pleasures of an empire of goods were reluctant to give uninhibited voice to rage.

The Reverend Benjamin Trumbull, a respected minister in Connecticut, expressed the emotional hold of soft colonialism as well as any of his contemporaries. At a moment when British taxation seemed to be leading to a major political confrontation, he addressed the people of New Haven. Like so many Americans, he wanted to avoid a crisis that might destroy the bonds of empire. "All men seem to glory in the riches, valour, honour, literary accomplishments, and various excellencies of their own country and nation," Trumbull explained. Anyone contemplating separation from Great Britain faced a difficult challenge, since "it is not easily that such a regard for their native land is obliterated, and the influence of it destroyed." Could colonists—no matter how angry about recent parliamentary legislation—seriously contemplate independence from "the country under whose laws and immunities, the religion, fortunes, and everything dear to their ancestors or to themselves, have been protected and defended. . . . Here are the companions, the guides and protectors of their youth."[21]

One of the more poignant expressions of colonial nostalgia comes, surprisingly, from Thomas Jefferson. A committee composed of Benjamin Franklin, John Adams, and other revolutionary leaders entrusted the young Virginian to draft a declaration of independence they could present to the full Continental Congress for approval. The choice was brilliant. After more than two centuries, we still celebrate Jefferson's inspired assertion that "all men are created equal, that they are endowed by their Creator with certain unalienable Rights, that among these are Life, Liberty and the pursuit of Happiness."

Because the promise of equality has proved so contentious in the United States since 1776, we ignore the draft that he actually submitted to the committee. That is a mistake. His words serve as a reminder of the ambivalence that colonists felt about separation from Great Britain. In fact, it reads like a lament that someone might have sent to a former lover. The tone is sentimental, an emotional cry of regret. In the "original rough draught," Jefferson reviewed the many instances when "our British brethren" have ignored "our repeated petitions" for fundamental constitutional rights. These efforts achieved nothing. American loyalty made no impression on the people of Great Britain. And so, with heavy heart, Jefferson continues, "we must endeavor to forget our former love for them, and to hold them as we hold the rest of mankind, enemies in war, in peace friends."

The colonial relationship—Franklin's "noble China Vase"—had once held such promise. Jefferson shares this sense of loss. "We might have been a free & a great people together; but a communication of grandeur & of freedom it seems is below their dignity." In this situation, the colonists find themselves spurned. Their only option is to "acquiesce in the necessity which pronounces our everlasting Adieu!"[22] The members of Congress may have shared Jefferson's reservations about separation, but they wisely revised his original statement. After all, Jefferson's sentimental declaration hardly contained the kind of spirited rhetoric military resistance requires.

Commentators on both sides of the Atlantic shared Jefferson's sentiments about separation from Great Britain. British administrators before the war insisted that the bonds between the Americans and the mother country were so strong that no one need worry about talk of independence. Thomas Pownall, for example, a former royal governor of Massachusetts, assured imperial policymakers during the 1760s that the colonists were really English people living on the other side of the Atlantic Ocean. "Their attachment to the protestant succession in the house of Hanover will ever stand unshaken," he explained, "and nothing can eradicate from their hearts their natural, almost mechanical, affection to Great Britain, which they conceive under no other sense, nor call by any other name, than that of *home.*"[23]

Pownall was no fool. Like many contemporaries, however, he conflated culture and politics. The colonists' highly praised affection for the imperial regime did nothing to discourage resistance to parliamentary taxation without representation. Even though the war frayed the bonds that Pownall saw as the foundation of imperial unity, these cultural ties survived the rejection of king and Parliament. Abigail Adams understood the foundation of the enduring relationship, a legacy of soft colonialism. A firm supporter of revolution and certainly no friend of Pownall, she affirmed his argument. In 1774—in other words, after revolutionary resistance had turned to violence in Boston—she maintained that America and Britain were "connected . . . by Blood, by commerce, by one common language, by one common religion as Protestants, and as good and loyal subjects of the same king."[24] This is not the language of genealogy or concern for distant relatives in the Old Country. Adams is making a sociological observation about the taken-for-granted cultural elements that had held imperial society together.

One additional comment on cultural tensions after independence brings us closer to the Henley trial. William Tudor, a prominent Massachusetts lawyer and the adjutant general at the court-martial, was asked in 1779 to give the annual Boston Massacre lecture. The event commemorated the people shot by British soldiers in 1770. Tudor had every reason to excoriate the British. But, like so many other Americans trying to make sense of cultural independence, he did not do so. He had no use for George III, of course, and in an attack that Paine might have admired, Tudor announced: "If a man in private life, finds his oldest son an idiot or a rascal, he may dispose of his estate among his other children: But if the heir apparent (in hereditary monarchies) to a crown, an inheritance in which millions are interested, turns out to be blockhead or a villain, still he must be King." Political separation from an aristocratic regime made common sense.

But, then, in the middle of the lecture, Tudor suddenly shifted the focus of his argument. A terrible king had destroyed a marvelous colonial relationship. He urged an audience that may have actually experienced the Massacre to turn their "eyes to that nation whom we once did love, and with whom we had yet been friends had not an unparalleled series of folly and cruelty compelled us to renounce this pleasing relation-ship." Could the Americans who had dumped the tea into Boston Harbor not remember the recent past when Great Britain was "an unrivalled figure" throughout the world? The mother country had been great "in commerce and in wealth. Not a corner of the earth but had witnesses of her achievements." Tudor could hardly contain his enthusiasm for the nation determined to destroy the United States. Great Britain's glory surpassed all previous empires: "Triumphant in war, not less distinguished in peace. In *most* of the polite, in *all* the useful arts and sciences, superior to her neighbours. In commerce unequalled; not a sea but bore, not a wind but wafted her countless ships, laden with the riches of the earth, and made her crowded ports the marts of the world."[25]

Widespread nostalgia for the former regime meant that almost everyone harbored conflicting sentiments about cultural independence. A person could at once enthusiastically support the creation of a new republic and at the same time desire British manufactured goods that had defined the good life under imperial rule. These tensions usually coexisted without serious disquiet. Reading a novel published in London or purchasing a few yards of woolen cloth did not indicate that a person regretted political separation from England. But occasionally the strain could not be ignored. During the war local controversies forced revolutionaries to confront the cultural challenge of independence, to discover what it meant to be no longer British in America. The court-martial of David Henley was such a moment. The trial brought out into the open lingering insecurities about whether the Americans were as civilized—as honorable—as the people they were fighting.

* * *

The events on Prospect Hill brought individuals together who under normal circumstances would have nothing to do with each other. Had Henley not assaulted a British prisoner, William Heath and John Burgoyne would not have argued so vehemently about the implications of American independence. Heath was a Roxbury farmer who rose through the ranks of the Continental Army. He never received a college education. What he knew about military affairs he learned from books. Above all, Heath never wavered in his support for national independence and a government based on the will of the people.

Burgoyne, Heath's adversary, represented an aristocratic society in which power and honor followed bloodlines. For six months—from November 1777 to April 1778—these generals took the measure of each other, negotiating, arguing, and threatening. Control of a huge prisoner-of-war camp compelled the American farmer and British aristocrat to sustain a stressful debate about national honor and responsibility. Henley's actions fueled their exchange; William Tudor defended the new republic in a dramatic court battle. Their lives initially became entangled during the British occupation of Boston in 1775, and to the surprise of all, after Burgoyne's defeat at Saratoga, they found themselves debating the responsibilities of independence in a small Massachusetts courtroom. The story begins with the British occupation of Boston.

• CHAPTER 2 •

Theater of War

The arrival of regular British troops on May 13, 1774, marked the start of a new coercive regime. The government dispatched them to America as a punishment for the destruction of the tea in Boston Harbor. The transformation of city life was sudden and dramatic. Overnight, Boston became an occupied city, a military outpost far from the imperial center, and by 1775, Boston looked much like those disturbingly familiar places throughout the modern world where a hostile army has seized control of civilian affairs.[1]

Through it all, the revolutionaries commanding the heights around Boston maintained high spirits. Within Boston, however, the military sparked anger and fear. Ordinary British troops established a large armed camp on the Commons; officers commandeered the homes of private citizens. Americans were assaulted in the streets; women endured insults. Underpaid soldiers, far from home and suspicious of the locals, engaged in petty theft. The days of occupation passed slowly, boredom, discontent, and privation defining the daily routine in a city under siege.

Within this troubled environment—so different from the soft colonialism that had defined the imperial system in earlier times—men who would later confront each other in a bizarre court-martial first took the full measure of each other. Burgoyne, Heath, and Henley could not have possibly foreseen the future confrontation, but at this moment, in a restive city, they formed strong impressions of those who opposed them, former friends identified now either as rebels or oppressors. As these men took stock of the situation, they made assessments of personal character and crass behavior that could not be erased. The process was wholly predictable. The intense experience of military occupation tested and then affirmed commitment to abstract values, giving the clash of cultures an emotional dimension.[2]

* * *

British administrators anticipated quashing the American rebellion with ease. As has occurred repeatedly throughout history, imperial authorities in distant capitals annoyed by colonial disobedience assumed that only overwhelming force would restore order. They believed compromise betrayed weakness. George III made it abundantly clear that he would brook no further resistance, and he was joined by a majority in Parliament demanding an abject apology for the destruction of the tea. General Thomas Gage seemed a promising figure to bring ungrateful Americans to heel. His bold rhetoric inspired confidence in London. During an audience with the king, Gage announced that the Americans "will be Lions, whilst we are Lambs, but if we take the resolute part, they will undoubtedly prove very meek." Since these were opinions that George wanted to hear, he concluded that Gage possessed the "character of an honest determined man."[3]

However convincing the general's rhetoric may have been, he did not live up to expectations in America. His military experience in Europe did not prepare him to contain a huge insurgency that put British troops at risk whenever they ventured into the Massachusetts countryside. And so, as Americans such as Heath and Henley fortified the hills around Boston, Gage watched and waited, begging for ever more support from England and frustrating the king's ministers, who demanded immediate results. Even before the embarrassing retreat from Concord in April 1775, they had concluded that Gage was not the man for the job. Lord North surveyed available options, and after a period of political maneuvering at court—aristocrats vying for preferment—he turned to three potentially more able generals to prod Gage to adopt a more aggressive military strategy. Generals Henry Clinton, William Howe, and John Burgoyne arrived on the *Cerberus*, a British warship, on May 25, 1775, almost a month before the debacle on Bunker Hill. The Americans were not impressed. These lines of doggerel appeared in a Boston newspaper: "Behold the *Cerberus* the Atlantic plough, Her precious cargo Burgoyne, Clinton, Howe. Bow, wow, wow."[4] Little changed. Whatever their military qualifications, the new generals could not remove the New England militiamen encircling Boston.

Burgoyne made no attempt to disguise his unhappiness in Boston. He witnessed the carnage on Bunker Hill from the city's North End, and although he avoided the criticism directed to General Howe—the officer who led charge after charge against American positions on a very hot day—Burgoyne quickly recognized that there was no glory to be had in this provincial port. Moreover, after the defeat, conditions in the city deteriorated rapidly. Everywhere one encountered desperate people searching for safety. Some of the refugees hoped to reach relatives in the Massachusetts interior; others, who supported the king, sought to join the loyalist community in Boston. British military officers were not prepared to deal with the situation. They struggled to find food and fuel for the regular soldiers. Not surprisingly, their apparent indifference—perhaps incompetence is the better word—undermined Gage's hope to restore imperial order.

What Burgoyne thought of the disruption of civilian life is unclear. Before sailing for Boston, he had a curious conversation with Thomas Hutchinson, the former royal governor of Massachusetts who emigrated to London in part to escape American detractors. Burgoyne asked questions about enforcing martial law in the colonies, assuming perhaps that the army could treat the rebels in a way unthinkable in England itself.[5] Nothing came of the idea. What greeted him in 1775 was the social chaos that is most often associated with the suffering of displaced civilians during a civil war.

Hannah Winthrop, who later provided key insights into the Henley trial, recorded what was happening. Unlike other commentators who concentrated on the movement of troops—American and British—she focused on the terrifying experiences of mothers and children, on the breakup of families. These were the experiences she and others associated with Burgoyne. In a letter written in May 1775, Winthrop, who was married to a leading Harvard professor, captured the sense of fear driving the refugee crisis. The incident occurred just after dinner. The Americans issued a general alarm. There were reports of fighting. Hannah and her husband managed to reach a safe house, which they discovered to their horror was "filled with women whose husbands were gone forth to meet the Assailants, 70 or 80 of these with numbers of Infant Children, Crying and agonizing for the Fate of their husbands." Scenes of this sort gave revolution a terrible reality that academic pamphlets about constitutional rights could never achieve. Two months later—after full-scale battles—Winthrop confessed, "My heart Bleeds for the people of Boston[,] my Blood boils with resentment at the Treatment they have met with from Gage." The destruction of the tea had brought a reign of "Barbarity," and then she asked rhetorically, "Can anything equal the distress of parents separated from their Children?"[6]

Winthrop's friend Abigail Adams bore witness to the same events. She had long expressed sympathy for the American cause, but the suffering of ordinary people transformed her into a zealous revolutionary. In a remarkable letter written to John Adams on July 25, 1775, Abigail asked why men of alleged integrity—the three newly arrived British generals—could become the agents of such violence. Although she was suspicious of Howe, she did not identify him as especially obnoxious. Clinton presented something of a mystery. He deserved the benefit of the doubt. "Clinton's General character very good," Abigail concluded, "and tis said he does not relish the Service he is sent upon."

About Burgoyne, Abigail had not the slightest doubt. She described him as mean and insensitive. What inflamed her ire was a story then circulating in Massachusetts. A woman—never identified—living in a house across the street from Burgoyne's temporary residence observed an act of wanton destruction. "She saw," Abigail explained, "raw meat cut and hacked upon her [the neighbor's] Mahogona Tables, and her superb damask curtain and cushings exposed to the rain as if they were of no value." These were the types of objects that Benjamin Franklin claimed had held soft colonialism together by a thread. Burgoyne was ridiculing a consumer economy that had long been dominated by women.

As frightened Americans sought safe havens, Burgoyne hacked away. According to Abigail, the explanation for such behavior was clear. More than any of the other British generals, Burgoyne lacked "Generosity, Virtue or Humanity." Language was not sufficient to provide "a true Idea of the Horrible wickedness of the Man. His designs are dark, his Dissimulation of the deepest die." Even more insulting, he professed obnoxious religious values, "when every action of his life is totally abhorrent to all Ideas of True Religion, Virtue or common Honesty." Of course, Abigail's character assessment begged the question, Was Burgoyne just an unusually hateful person, or was he simply a typical representative of an arrogant, aristocratic culture determined to inflict pain on the Americans? She concluded with an observation that people have repeated often when wickedness threatens society. It is "really to be lamented when a Man possessed of one spark of virtue should be drawn aside, and disgrace himself and posterity."[7]

* * *

Years before American protest sparked an imperial crisis, a fellow officer commissioned a portrait of Burgoyne by the acclaimed artist Joshua Reynolds. At that moment Burgoyne was just entering middle age. He seems, in the portrait, remarkably self-composed, robust, staring out at the viewer with a sense of empowerment often associated with aristocratic privilege. Whether Reynolds captured the sitter's true character can never be known. The painting does suggest that Abigail Adam's vilification of Burgoyne may have been excessive. She was certainly not a neutral observer when it came to judging British officers. Still, she had a point. Conversations about Burgoyne almost always triggered a cascade of adjectives: He struck contemporaries as clever, charming, mercurial, ambitious, insecure, opportunistic, and courageous. The use of so many descriptive words to characterize him suggests that he developed a protean persona and that, depending on the social situation in which he found himself, he revealed facets of his character designed to further his own immediate ends. Since Burgoyne achieved modest fame in London as a playwright, working with celebrities such Richard Sheridan and David Garrick, it is highly likely that he imagined his own life as a player on a public stage where he could manipulate the scene. But then, perhaps the flood of adjectives Burgoyne inspired was merely a carapace he cultivated, masking the possibility that his most cherished value was simply getting ahead.[8]

Burgoyne was born in Bedfordshire, England, in February 1723—about a decade earlier than his American nemesis George Washington. Burgoyne's parents claimed solid gentry status, although at the time of his birth they were experiencing financial difficulties. Many years later mean-spirited rumors circulated suggesting that he was the illegitimate son of Baron Bingley, a powerful political figure during the reign of Queen Anne. There was no truth to the story, but it did remind Burgoyne's catty contemporaries that he was not in fact a member of the aristocracy and, therefore, never in the same social class as were his military rivals Howe and Clinton. Although one hesitates to assign causes for a person's behavior, one could argue plausibly that Burgoyne's insecurity about his own

General John Burgoyne, Joshua Reynolds, ca. 1766. Oil on canvas, 50 × 39⅞ in. (Image © The Frick Collection)

social standing fueled a constant drive for public recognition. His excessive ambition—a way of acting that was widely observed and condemned at the time—figured in his willingness to take personal risks that repeatedly put his reputation in jeopardy.

One impulsive decision involved Burgoyne's marriage. He fell in love with a fifteen-year-old girl who happened to be the daughter of the Earl of Derby. This wealthy and politically influential patriarch expected to have his way in all things touching the family. The eager suitor did not fit into his plans, and predictably, when Burgoyne eloped with Charlotte in 1751, Derby disinherited his daughter, leaving the young couple without the resources needed to maintain a high social profile. When the Burgoynes announced the birth of a daughter several years later, however, the father relented. The reconciliation solved Burgoyne's immediate financial difficulties. But even with access to his wife's money, he always spent more on gambling and entertainment than he could afford.

Like many ambitious men of his social background, Burgoyne followed a military career. In eighteenth-century England, a person eager to become an officer in the army had to purchase the position. The price was not insubstantial, and Burgoyne often had trouble raising the money. But he persevered, slowly making his way through the ranks. There was no doubt that he possessed genuine talent for organization and command. The soldiers who served with him expressed universal respect for his leadership, and he put forward several innovative ideas about training. During the Seven Years' War, Burgoyne saw action on the coast of France and, later, in Portugal, where he led an attack that turned the tide of battle. But when the war was over and Britain no longer needed a large army, he struggled to secure a regular place. He boldly—some said shamelessly—lobbied the prime minister, the Earl of Bute, for an appointment that he felt he deserved. Initially turned down, he badgered other leading government ministers. They finally grew tired of his persistence, naming him a full colonel. By 1772 Burgoyne's charm and self-promoting yielded rewards. He became a major general, a promotion that gave him the same rank as Howe and Clinton.

Rising military officers who enjoyed the patronage of an elite family—and in the eighteenth century this meant possession of large amounts of land and control over scores of tenants—often entered politics. Burgoyne was no exception. In 1761 the freeholders of Midhurst elected him to a seat in Parliament. They really did not have a choice. The Earl of Derby simply announced the name of his favored candidate, and the locals did his bidding. The system almost backfired in 1768, when Derby put Burgoyne forward in a rare contested election, and during a heated contest, Burgoyne appeared among the voters in full uniform carrying two guns. His theatrics may have intimidated the opposition. When the losing group later sued Burgoyne in a Crown court, however, he lost and had to paid a huge fine. No matter. The prime minister at the time not only paid the penalty but also provided the clubbable general with a handsome sinecure, the governorship of Fort William in Scotland. Obtaining a position that required no work became a sensitive issue much later during the American trial. As a member of Parliament, Burgoyne seldom spoke, and with rare exception he voted as his benefactor desired. When he actually participated in debate—as he did several times on the eve of the American Revolution—other members found his performances boring, even pompous. Horace Walpole, a well-connected commentator possessing a vituperative wit, declared Burgoyne "a vain, very ambitious man, with a half-understanding which was worse than none."[9]

A year before Burgoyne sailed for Boston, he organized an amazing pageant. It was the type of event reminding the less fortunate members of society that the rich really were different. In honor of the engagement of one of the Derbys, Burgoyne wrote *The Maid of the Oaks*. He called the work a play, but in fact the entire production defied easy description. The text is almost unreadable today. The loosely scripted spectacle required scores of performers, musicians, games, and nymphs hanging from trees. It also cost a very large amount of money. Celebrities loved the show, and *The Maid* soon appeared on the London stage. Curiously, two editions of the play were printed in Philadelphia in 1777.[10] Since General Howe then controlled the city, the publication may have been directed at British officers, but Americans in the audience may have wondered at such extravagance at a moment when Great Britain was willing to go to war over colonial taxation. And, of course, for the people in Boston who closely followed the news from England, the extravaganza was forever associated with Burgoyne.

In 1772 Burgoyne celebrated his fiftieth birthday. The moment called for a difficult self-appraisal. He had no regular command, and unless he obtained a posting soon, his military prospects seemed bleak. The challenge triggered a charm offensive. As the American crisis loomed, he lobbied friends in government. In public, he sometimes adopted a coy persona, as if he had no desire to take an active part in putting down a colonial rebellion. No one believed him. In any case, his immediate goal was obtaining a position that provided public recognition of his accomplishments, real or imagined, as well as full command over the British troops sent to Boston. He succeeded in persuading the king to give him a higher rank in the army, but much to his annoyance, Burgoyne found himself in America serving not only under General Gage but also on equal footing with Howe and Clinton.

Before sailing for the colonies on April 24, 1775, Burgoyne delivered several speeches in Parliament. They provide insight into his core political principles. What did he expect to achieve in America? Since he did not produce a memoir or preserve most of his personal correspondence, one has to rely on parliamentary records and newspaper accounts to understand his thinking about the war. Of course, it was not only the English who followed the news. Reports about the man so eager to end the rebellion eventually reached American readers curious about the character of the British general.

Burgoyne declared before the House of Commons that the only things that he cared for were military honor and fealty to the king. When called to fight in a "foreign war"—the term alone suggests that he did not view the Americans as fully English—"The soldier draws his sword with alacrity; the cause in which he engages rests between God and his Prince; and he wants no other excitements to his duty, than such as the glory of his Country, personal honour, and just ambition will suggest."[11] Burgoyne could not resist describing his own sense of self-sacrifice in histrionic fashion. He informed George III that he imagined the possibility of his own demise fighting for king and country. "Whenever this letter shall be delivered to your Majesty," he explained, "the writer of it will be no more. It may therefore be esteemed an address from beyond the grave, and under that idea I am persuaded your Majesty will consider with indulgence both the matter and the expression." Sounding like a noble Roman warrior on the eve of battle, he urged the king to protect the interests of Lady Charlotte, Burgoyne's "weak" widow.[12]

About the glorious political achievements of eighteenth-century Great Britain, Burgoyne echoed the ideas of the country's ruling class. In an exchange with General Charles Lee, a leading Continental officer who had once served in the British army, Burgoyne exclaimed, "I have, like you entertained from infancy a Veneration for public Liberty. I have likewise regarded the British Constitution as the best Safeguard of that Blessing to be found in the History of Mankind."[13] There is no reason to doubt his sincerity. He situated himself within a commonly accepted narrative celebrating the Glorious Revolution (1688–89) as the event liberating the English people from the tyranny of Stuart monarchs—specifically James II—and instituting a new regime in which kings observed the rule of law and accepted the supremacy of Parliament. These assumptions were known as the Whig interpretation of history. It was a complacent story justifying to England's leaders why the aristocracy ruled the land.

In a statement an American revolutionary could have written, Burgoyne insisted, "I am no Stranger to the Doctrines of Mr. [John] Locke and other Advocates for the Rights of Mankind, upon the Compacts always implied between the governing and governed and the Right of Resistance in the Latter when the Compact shall be violated as to leave no other Means of Redress."[14] For colonists who claimed that they were in fact exercising the "Right of Resistance," Burgoyne's declaration must have come as a surprise. Had a Boston publisher not recently brought out the first American edition of John Locke's *Second Treatise of Government* (originally 1689), which informed the colonists, "Perhaps there never was a Time since the Discovery of this New World, when the People of all Ranks everywhere show'd so eager a Spirit of Inquiry into the Nature of their Rights and Privileges, as this Day"?[15] Moreover, the revolutionaries' new battle flag carried the phrase "An Appeal to Heaven," words that came straight from Locke's radical defense of the Glorious Revolution. Burgoyne drew upon a shared political heritage.

Of course, Burgoyne was no revolutionary. He declared in no uncertain terms that restive colonists had nothing in common with the members of Parliament who sent the Stuarts packing a century earlier. The Americans were whining over a matter of taxation. Their cause did not involve a fundamental constitutional issue. He had no patience with anyone who doubted the supremacy of Parliament. That institution defined the law. "The vital principle of the [British] constitution, in which It moves and has being," Burgoyne insisted, "is the supremacy of the King in Parliament—a compound, indefinite, indefeasible power, coeval with the origins of empire, and coextensive over all its parts."[16]

When colonists asserted that they would accept no taxation without representation, they challenged the fundamental principles of the dominant Whig interpretation of history. Indeed, Burgoyne believed that the Americans had abandoned the basic principles that explained Britain's rise to a great world power. Confronted with ungrateful colonists, the military representatives of king and Parliament were obliged to bring about the total destruction of "the compleatest system of Tyranny that ever God in his displeasure suffer'd for a time to be exercised over a froward and stubborn Generation."[17] These were the kind of ideas that the imperial rulers have expressed about their dependent subjects for centuries. If only colonized peoples in Asia and Africa knew what was in their best interests, they would not only obey their sovereign but also realize the errors of their ways—even the inferiority of their own cultures. It comes as no surprise to learn that Burgoyne informed Parliament, "I look upon America as our child, which we have already spoilt by too much indulgence." As for the British army in Boston, "We are contending in this crisis for the fate of the British Empire."[18]

Boston was a disaster for Burgoyne. He had expected the posting to enhance his military reputation in the eyes of the king's ministers. Instead, the new arrival found himself taking orders from General Gage, who seemed overwhelmed by the unexpected resolve of American militiamen. After the embarrassing setbacks at Concord and then at Bunker Hill, Gage advanced no credible plans for pacifying the countryside. Burgoyne might have bided his time, waiting for his superiors in London to develop a new strategy. But he lacked patience. He dispatched a flood of letters criticizing his colleagues. Burgoyne openly mocked the slow-moving Gage. "In the military," Burgoyne observed, "I believe him capable of figuring upon ordinary and given lines of conduct; but his mind has not resources for great, and sudden, and hardy exertions, which spring self-suggested in extraordinary characters, and generally overbear all opposition."[19]

What could be done to save the situation? The king and Lord North, the first minister, could come to a timely realization that Burgoyne's talents were being wasted as a junior officer in Boston. After all, he explained, "My rank only serves to place me in a motionless, drowsy, irksome medium, or rather vacuum, too low for the honour of command, too high for that of execution." Everything had gone wrong in America. He even blamed the regular British soldiers for the defeat at Bunker Hill. "Discipline," he reported, "not to say courage was wanting." More troublesome, the Red Coats had deserted their officers in the midst of battle, and he believed "all the wounds of the officers were not received from the enemy." Fortunately, Burgoyne knew exactly what needed to be done. The British government should hire a large number of foreign fighters. This new force could "begin their operations up the Hudson River; another army composed of old disciplined troops and party of Canadians to act from Canada." This grand army required only "a large levy of Indians, and a supply of arms for the blacks, to awe the southern provinces." If London accepted his brilliant scheme, he was confident that the whole war might be over "in one campaign."[20] Perhaps this assertion was just bravado. Two months after the disaster on Bunker Hill, Burgoyne reflected, "I believe in most states of the world as well as in our own, that respect, and control, and subordination of government . . . depends in a great measure upon the idea that trained troops are invincible against any numbers or any position of undisciplined rabble; and this idea was a little in suspense since the 19th of April."[21] Like so many overly confident military figures throughout history, he seems to have soon forgotten his own insight into the indomitable character of insurgency.

To relieve his boredom, Burgoyne managed to make matters worse—at least, for the people of Boston who had grown weary of living with an army of occupation. He ordered the Old South Church to be turned into a riding school. British officers apparently needed to practice their equestrian skills in an indoor facility. The impetuous decision would come back to haunt him some years later when he became a prisoner of war.

Locals were horrified by how British troops had desecrated a church, tearing out the ancient pews and destroying valuable historic records. Would soldiers stationed on English soil have engaged in such outrageous behavior? In his diary Deacon Newell assessed the damage: "The pulpit, pews and seats, all cut to pieces, and carried off in the most savage manner as can ever be expressed." Despite his hesitancy, he gave full expression to his anger: "The beautiful carved pew, with the silk furniture, of Deacon Hubbard's, was taken down and carried to ________'s house by an officer, and made a hog-stye." There was no question in Newell's mind about who was responsible. "The above," he recorded in the diary, "was effected by the solicitation of General Burgoyne."[22] Other witnesses—including one who entered Boston soon after the British departed from Boston in March 1776—verified Newell's observations. "I went to view the Old South Church, a spacious brick building near the center of town," wrote James Thacher in his *Military Journal.* "It has been for more than a century consecrated to the service of religion, and many eminent divines have in its pulpit labored in teaching the ways of righteousness and truth. But during the late siege the inside of it was entirely destroyed by the British."[23]

As everyone knew, Burgoyne's actions involved more than an attack on a church. Since he identified the building with revolutionary protest, his decision to turn it into a riding school represented an act of political revenge. After all, the Old South was where Joseph Warren, who died during the Battle of Bunker Hill, gave a fiery public lecture commemorating the Americans killed by British troops during the so-called Boston Massacre. It was also where Benjamin Franklin was baptized before he moved to Philadelphia. And it was here that Phillis Wheatley, the acclaimed Black poet, worshipped. Burgoyne was surely aware of the protest meetings held there in 1775, but perhaps he was ignorant of the church's long history in the city. The people who lived there were not.[24] More than any other aspect of the occupation, this assault reminded Americans that they were colonials, second-class subjects in the empire, not quite British. Many of them were not yet prepared to cut the thread of soft colonialism, but the memory of Burgoyne's atrocity accelerated them along the way.

For William Heath, whose ancestors had fled England during the 1630s to escape religious persecution, Burgoyne's boorish behavior was unacceptable. It was personal. He insulted the history and traditions of New England. Of course, at that moment Burgoyne would have paid no attention to a rather ordinary man who now served as a revolutionary officer. That was a mistake. Burgoyne would soon learn that a British aristocrat could not intimidate a Roxbury farmer.

* * *

For the author of an engaging memoir of the American Revolution, General William Heath suffered an undeserved humiliation.[25] When his work was first published in 1798, it carried a portrait of a handsome military officer. Sadly, even though the image bore his name, it was not in fact Heath. As a Boston press was turning out finished volumes, an editor discovered that "the portrait is really that of Gen. Wilkinson." To make matters worse—at least, for the long-term reputation of Heath—James Wilkinson was later exposed as a spy for Spain. Theodore Roosevelt claimed, "In all our history, there is no more despicable character."[26] Other prints claiming to be Heath survive—one is reproduced here—but they may have been produced after his death or from memory.

Post-revolutionary print of General William Heath, by H. Williams. (New York Public Library Digital Collections, Miriam and Ira D. Wallach Division of Art, Prints and Photographs)

Although Heath achieved modest prosperity during his long life (1737–1814), he never commissioned a court painter to capture his likeness. He may not have even been aware of Joshua Reynolds. The aristocratic society in which Burgoyne circulated had little appeal for Heath, who prided himself in being a New England farmer. Heath's larger significance is that he helps restore to the revolutionary story an element that often goes missing. He provides a personal, even emotional understanding of how a middling sort of person came to support resistance. Heath was not a firebrand such as Samuel Adams or John Hancock or an intellectual guide to resistance such as John Adams. Rather, he was more typical of most fervent, taken-for-granted revolutionaries who were in fact absolutely necessary in sustaining the fight for independence.

War has always brought out talents in people who otherwise might have remained obscure. The American Revolution is no exception. In Heath's case, the challenge of unanticipated responsibility transformed a well-to-do farmer into a trusted general. He responded to the breakdown of the British Empire in ways that persuaded friends and neighbors that he possessed special abilities, even that ineffable attribute known as leadership. David Ramsay, an officer in the Continental Army and accomplished historian, marveled at this process: "The great bulk of those, who were active instruments of carrying on the revolution, were self-made, industrious men. Those who by their own exertions, had established or laid a foundation for establishing personal independence, were most generally trusted, and most successfully employed in establishing that of their country."[27] Heath was a genuine revolutionary, as much as were Samuel Adams or Patrick Henry. He was precisely the kind of person required to sustain the momentum of rebellion—loyal, competent, a trusted link between celebrated leaders such as George Washington and the ordinary soldiers who remain largely anonymous.

Although Heath apparently never commissioned a portrait, he left a fascinating word picture that reveals a complex character. He strives throughout the *Memoirs*—one of very few personal accounts of the war written by a Continental officer—to play down his own accomplishments. In the opening pages, he offers a remarkably self-deprecating sketch of his own physical appearance. Writing in the third person, Heath claims to be "of middle stature, light complexion, very corpulent, and bald-headed." He protests that he never intended to share his military experiences with the public. He certainly wanted to avoid seeming too "ostentatious." But friends and family insisted he put pen to paper. "The pressing importunity of very many," Heath observed, "is the sole reason of their appearance at this time."[28]

Unlike many of his more famous colleagues—John and Samuel Adams, for example—Heath never attended Harvard College. His lack of a formal degree may help to explain why his tone occasionally strikes the reader as defensive, as if he knows his style lacks academic gravitas and does not really care. "Although the following pages are not decorated with the flowers of Greece or Rome," Heath explains, "and for their diction cannot claim the patronage of the learned, they contain a slate of facts in detail."[29] At the time, people commented on "the republican simplicity of his manners." A nineteenth-century historian of Roxbury reported local gossip that Heath "occasionally drove to church in his ox-team—perhaps intended as a hint to his more aristocratic neighbors, whose carriages were of a showy and stylish description."[30] However pedestrian he may have regarded the prose—most modern readers will not share his view—he insists that he has done his research as fully as possible. If he has made mistakes, so be it: "There are doubtless many errors. It is the lot of man to be fallible."[31]

While a large section of the *Memoirs* focuses on his confrontation with Burgoyne, Heath opens with several comments about the Revolution that help us understand better his behavior during the court-martial of David Henley. One remark reminds us of the ambivalence even the most dedicated revolutionary felt about national independence. Heath candidly admits that separation need not have occurred. Great Britain and the colonies had enjoyed a mutually satisfactory relationship—a regime of soft colonialism—but the Parliament changed the rules. It introduced an "impolitic exercise of power, thereby alienating the affections of the Colonists, and rousing in their breasts those innate principles of liberty which nature hath implanted."[32]

Then, as if memories of a lost empire stirred mixed feelings, Heath voiced an opinion many readers would have shared. Had it not been for Britain's "severity of conduct, [the colonists] would have much longer reposed on the bosom of a mother, and even have spurned the idea of separation." Like other revolutionaries such as Thomas Jefferson, Heath tempered cultural nostalgia with pragmatic adjustment to unfolding events. In 1772 he advanced another, more defiant narrative, one that pictured the American people taking on responsibility for a new political world: "Our pious forefathers died with the pleasing hope that we, their children, should live free, let none, as they would answer it another day, disturb the ashes of those heroes by selling their birthright."[33]

Heath's patriotism—a word that unfortunately has become synonymous with modern flag-waving chauvinism—drew energy from his own family history. This is not surprising. After all, the emotional commitment to revolution always involved more than a defense of abstract principles such as freedom and liberty. Of course, these ideas motivated people to sacrifice a great deal for a cause that involved thirteen separate states. But general notions of freedom and liberty took on different meanings in different contexts. Regional histories and traditions did not necessarily compete with national narratives of resistance to imperial power. Rather, they usually complemented shared stories about the colonists' road to independence, and thereby served to justify participation in a larger cause.

Sometimes tensions have developed between a regional and national sense of identity—as Southerners have demonstrated for several centuries—but for Heath that was not the case. His love of a family-owned farm in Roxbury anchored his devotion first to New England, and then, by extension, to the United States.[34] The same sentiments informed George Washington's longing during the war and his presidency to return to Mount Vernon and John Adams's constant concern when he was doing the country's business about crops and harvests in his beloved Braintree.[35]

Although Heath was raised a "farmer, of which profession he is yet passionately fond," it was the land itself that anchored identity.[36] Possession of property situated him in a chronicle that began when the Puritans first arrived in Massachusetts. For him, New England's revolutionary history could be traced back to 1632, when the original Heaths decided that they could no longer endure religious persecution in England. General Heath took pride in being "descended from an ancient family in Roxbury . . . and is of the fifth generation of the family who have inherited the same real estate (taken up in the state of nature), not large but fertile and pleasantly situated."[37] Heath failed to note the Native Americans' prior possession of the area, but that is not how most New Englanders at the time perceived the spread of civilization.

The Reverend Amos Adams, a highly respected minister in Roxbury, reinforced Heath's sense of how regional history shaped revolutionary identity. In a remarkable fast day sermon delivered in 1769 in the local church, Adams recounted the story of New England's providentially guided development since John Winthrop and his fellow Puritans founded Boston in 1630. The published title of Adams's lecture is daunting, *A Concise, Historical View of the Perils, Hardships, Difficulties, and Discouragements Which Have Attended the Planting and Progressive Improvements of New-England,* and one cannot but admire the patience of his parishioners as he read sixty-nine pages of text. Heath was one of them. Adams confirmed what he and others in the community took for granted.[38]

More to the point, drawing on New England's religious history—the assurance that its people enjoyed a special relation with God—Adams justified political resistance to tyranny. His message made protest a moral obligation. This theologically based message is significant, because it illuminates Heath's uncompromising fight for independence. Modern explanations for the mobilization of the American people on the eve of the Revolution tend to discount the role of religion in energizing resistance to Great Britain. This is a mistake. It assumes that religious conviction is a separate analytic category from political ideology. But in fact, in terms of emotional commitment to the rejection of imperial rule, the two were mutually supportive. The certainty that New England's God expected true believers to defend liberty had as much impact on the behavior of ordinary revolutionaries as did the legal and constitutional tracts of the time. Of course, Heath and his Roxbury neighbors shared Burgoyne's esteem for the Glorious Revolution and eighteenth-century Britain's constitution, but they wove that self-congratulatory narrative into a story of their own.[39]

Adams provided the Roxbury congregation with a history marked by courage, self-reliance, and piety. For a revolutionary generation the message was clear. "Liberty is the most ardent wish of a brave and noble people," the minister declared. "They bear the yoke with reluctance; and never fail to improve the first opportunity to cast it off." And, now, history seemed to be repeating itself. The first colonists had not wanted to leave the comforts of England, but Archbishop William Laud and other leaders of the Anglican Church had driven them to "this howling wilderness." But exile had worked out. The New Englanders endured wars with the Native Americans, and even when the enemy seemed to gain the advantage, no one in the mother country offered the colonists support. James II ignored their suffering. "The heart of a licentious prince was hardened to all their distresses," Adams recounted. During more recent times, the New Englanders had prospered: "We have had many difficulties, hardships, and discouragements, [and still] we are increased, from very small and feeble beginnings, until we are become a very considerable people." Success certainly did not warrant complacence. A renewed threat of tyranny served as a reminder that "this country was first sought and settled as an Asylum for liberty, civil and religious: and it is worthy of observation that the abettors of arbitrary power, and ecclesiastical tyranny, have, all along, been enemies of New England." Adams's description of the region as a "country" in 1769 reveals just how deeply a sense of independence had taken root in Massachusetts. And it comes as no surprise that Adams—a zealous revolutionary—died from an illness contracted while visiting American soldiers after the Battle of Bunker Hill.[40]

In 1774—after the British government sent an army of occupation to punish Boston for the destruction of the tea—Heath attended a sermon delivered by the Reverend John Lathrop before the members of the Ancient and Honorable Artillery Company. We know that Heath was in attendance, because he was an officer in this special military organization first chartered in 1638.[41] Lathrop's words were far more incendiary than those of Adams five years earlier; the political climate had changed. Citing the works of John Locke and Scripture, he advanced a hypothetical warning—or, stated differently, he asked how a liberty-loving people should react to tyranny? Lathrop's zealous rhetoric anticipated that of Thomas Paine. "To pretend the precepts of the New Testament require us to yield a quiet and peaceable subjection to the insults of a cruel, ignorant wretch, who might possibly make his way to the throne, by murder and rebellion, would be to blaspheme the word of God," Lathrop informed the American officers. And if one turned to British history, one encountered many examples of "despotic rulers who have been put to an untimely death, or drove from their seats of government by the people."[42]

Lathrop argued that subjects who resist tyranny deserved respect. Almost a year before the Battles of Lexington and Concord, he insisted: "We may and ought, to resist, even make war against those rulers who leap the bounds prescribed them by the constitution, and attempt to oppress and enslave the subjects, is a principle on which the great revolutions which have taken place in our nation can be justified." Although Lathrop observed that no one in his audience could predict the outcome of the current imperial crisis, he imagined the embarrassment of some future historian having to confess that "this generation . . . tho' naturally fond of liberty, and tenacious of those rights . . . at length bowed their shoulders to bear and become servants into tribute." There was still time for Americans to revive "their love of freedom and their religion." Heath agreed, knowing full well at that moment that the burden of resistance might fall on him. Lathrop paid a price. British regulars destroyed his Boston church for firewood.[43]

As relations with Parliament deteriorated, people in Roxbury turned to Heath, first as a member of the local committee of safety and then as a military officer. After he was elected to the Massachusetts Assembly in the early 1770s, his neighbors appealed to him to defend "the rights and privileges of British subjects." He gained the respect of other members of the legislature more as a reliable supporter of other more outspoken colleagues such as Samuel Adams, John Hancock, and James Warren than as a leader in the intensifying protests against British colonial policy. About his own radical beliefs, there was no doubt. In 1772—a year before the destruction of the tea in Boston Harbor—Heath wrote a report for the town of Roxbury that urged the community to resist British oppression.[44]

Although there was little to distinguish Heath from a growing cadre of middle-level revolutionaries throughout Massachusetts, he knew a great deal more about military strategy than did the colony's political leaders. Why a self-styled Roxbury farmer would develop such an interest is not known. In the *Memoirs* he notes in passing that "from his childhood he was remarkably fond of military exercises, which passion grew up with him, and led him to procure and attentively to study every military treatise in the English language which was attainable." Heath built up an impressive library. In a passage expressing an uncharacteristic sense of pride, Heath declared that his research coupled with "a strong memory, rendered him fully acquainted with the theory of war in all its branches and duties, from the private soldier to the Commander in Chief."[45]

Despite his inability to read French or German, Heath's favorite authors shared insights gained from large-scale campaigns in continental Europe. He was especially fond of the works of Jacques Antoine Hippolyte, comte de Guibert (1743–1790), a widely respected French general who in 1770 published *Essai general de tactique*. Fortunately for Heath, the work was quickly translated into English. Guibert called for major military reforms. A critic of large, slow-moving armies that dominated eighteenth-century European battlefields, he recommended smaller, more mobile units. Of even greater significance in shaping Heath's ideas were the writings of Frederick the Great (1712–1786), king of Prussia. What impressed Heath were not the details of Frederick's victories over the Austrians or even the political tensions that triggered frequent dynastic wars. Rather, he praised Frederick for being a proponent of harsh but effective military discipline. According to the Prussian ruler, "Many soldiers can be governed only with sternness and occasionally with severity. If discipline fails to keep them in check, they are apt to commit the crudest excesses. Since they greatly outnumber their superiors, they can be held in check only through fear."[46]

For New England militiamen who elected their own officers and often viewed training days as an invitation for strong drink, Frederick's authoritarian principles were a nonstarter.[47] Heath knew that, but as a self-taught military tactician, he made a try. Often sounding like a Cassandra, he wrote a series of newspaper essays before the Revolution that aimed at teaching American soldiers how to resist an invasion by a foreign enemy, the French or the Spanish, but his readers surely knew that Heath had Great Britain in mind. Appearing in the *Boston Gazette* (1771) over the pen name "A Military Countryman," Heath's first article warned that the face of war had changed greatly since the first colonists confronted Native American adversaries. By the mid-eighteenth century, however, the population density of Massachusetts had increased. Towns had replaced open land and forests. In the early times, soldiers had relied on "firing from ambuscade." Tactics then depended on utilizing "closely woody places, where you have trees, rocks, logs, &c. to screen you."[48]

A frontier strategy was no longer adequate for the demands of modern warfare. Moreover, the problem was now more pressing than ever, largely because complacent New Englanders refused to adopt new practices. In fact, the Massachusetts militia had become an embarrassment. Instead of well-regulated local units, Heath encountered "regiments and companies without officers; or, if they have them, generally careless, unconcerned and ignorant of their duty." What Massachusetts needed—and this advice was published in Boston's leading journal four years before actual fighting began—was a radical shift in how people viewed military security. Heath insisted that "something more regular and uniform must be performed on the sea-coast, and in the old settled towns."[49]

The threat was real enough—at least in Heath's opinion. The major problem was not Spain or France, but Great Britain. The logic of Heath's argument was strained, but he wanted to make what was essentially a political point. If by chance the "enemies of Britain" concluded "they have a very particular advantage from a suppos'd disaffection in the colonies occasion'd by the cruel treatment they have for a number [of] years had from her," Heath warned, then the colonists would be well advised to protect themselves. They should immediately build castles and forts to protect New England ports and move weapons to safe inland depots. Self-reliance required something more. Inspired by Frederick the Great, Heath put his faith in a defense organized around a "well-regulated militia."[50] How seriously British officials in Massachusetts reacted to this article is not known. In all probability they concluded that an ill-trained militia represented no immediate danger. They certainly did not appreciate that a disaffected colonial officer such as Heath was making plans for an insurgency.

By late 1774 the military situation had changed dramatically. With a British army occupying Boston, theoretical advice about tactics and strategy seemed less relevant. New England's stone walls were no longer deemed a problem. After all, Heath asserted, when the enemy came, American fighters would discover "Nature *and* convenience has formed your country for defense—believe me it may be defended almost inch by inch, your whole country has *breast works already erected against small arms—every stone wall and log fence is a breast work.*"[51] As the infamous British retreat from Concord demonstrated, Heath was more correct about the military value of stone walls than he was about Frederick the Great's advocacy of discipline based on fear.

Confronted with the prospect of armed violence, Heath changed his tone. Writing as "A Military Countryman" in September 1774, Heath no longer chastised complacency. His approach seems more like that of a coach whose team is facing a much stronger opponent. He encouraged the ordinary soldiers of New England, assuring them that they should trust their own abilities to beat the odds. "The God of nature has formed you perhaps equal to any people on earth, both to *courage, strength,* and *genius,* you abound with *rough diamonds,* nothing more is wanting than they be *polished,*" he assured them. Experience suggested that "providence has put it in the power of the people of *America* . . . if *united,* to do *themselves justice.*"[52] Lest readers misinterpret his words as treasonous, Heath insisted that he was not advocating independence.

The loss of liberty, however, could never be tolerated. The time had come to defend freedom even if that involved death in combat. In a moving closing passage, he told untested militiamen that they might become martyrs to the American cause. Loss of life was a noble sacrifice:

> May God more abundantly endow you with *wisdom, skill* and *fortitude,* and may you do valiantly for God and the *cities* of your God—and should it be the fate of any of you to lose your lives in defense of your *country* and its *liberties,*—should you be forced to it, remember that *posterity* will reap the *fruits* of your *sufferings* (as you do of those worthy ancestors, many of whom watered the ground on which you tread with their *blood!*) will and rise up and call you blessed.[53]

The writing of the "Military Countryman" received unexpected praise more than thirty years after its original publication. In 1807 John Adams—retired from the presidency—reviewed newspaper articles that had appeared on the eve of independence. Heath's essays merited special praise. Adams wrote to Heath, who had returned to his beloved Roxbury, explaining that he has relished these pieces "like the best of old wine." While reading them, "I seemed to be conversing with an old Friend, whom I had not seen for an Age," and was greatly impressed by the military insights "produced by a young Officer of our own so long before the revolutionary War commenced." Reflecting on the events of the previous decades, Adams stated that the United States greatly needed leaders such as Heath. As it had turned out, republican governments were just as prone to engage in war as were monarchies: "There is always in a Democracy some Themistocles or Pericles, some Alexander Hamilton or Aaron Burr, weary of the dull pursuits of civil Life and impatient to be at the head of affairs."[54] How much the references to ancient Greek leaders resonated with Heath is hard to judge. He seems to have viewed the Old Testament as a more reliable guide.

Heath welcomed the compliments. How he reacted to Adams's gentle criticism is not known. The former president explained to his fellow revolutionary that modern Americans—people who had established a new republic—should be careful before advocating the creation of a military system of the type championed by Frederick the Great. Placing too much power in the hands of an aggressive military leader threatened the very democratic principles that had once energized the American Revolution. "The King of Prussia's Maxim is a remnant of the old System," Adams counseled. All too often, over-mighty military leaders established a privileged order of men who believed that they alone "ought to enjoy [a country's] principal honours, Dignities and Emoluments." Fortunately, in Adams's opinion, recent events had "produced an entire Revolution in the Sentiments of Mankind." As a result, the autocratic regime Frederick had envisioned "will not Succeed in this age either in America or Europe."[55] It is doubtful that Adams's faith in a republican government persuaded Heath. The old general still admired well-drilled soldiers.

Heath served in a number of military positions, first in the colonial system, and then, after Great Britain sent an army to Boston, in the newly organized American army. The transition was easy. He always defined his service through the lens of local and regional interests. People regarded him as a competent, reliable officer, though not a charismatic one. His reputation as a serious student of strategy earned respect, and, perhaps more important for his eventual rise to a position of command, he showed up when others were uncertain how best to mobilize military resources. After the British retreated from Concord in April 1775, Heath helped bring order to the various militia units that were acting pretty much on their own. Later that year he was named a brigadier general in the newly formed Continental Army.

What do we make of a genuine revolutionary such as Heath? No one questioned his commitment to the American cause. But it is striking—especially at a moment when we are experiencing extreme ideological division—that the content of Heath's patriotism was remarkably thin. Unlike other revolutionaries who have overthrown established regimes over the last two centuries—in China, Russia, and France, for example—he seemed to have no clear sense of what resistance could or should achieve. He did not advocate killing priests. He showed no deep-seated resentment about economic inequities. He may have believed that the current British government was thoroughly corrupt. Other Americans apparently subscribed to conspiracy theories about dark plots in England designed to curtail colonial rights, but Heath never mentioned such nefarious plans. Nor did Heath envision the creation of a new republic founded on the will of the people. Indeed, in the same newspaper essay in which he appealed to the blood of martyrs, he also confessed, "I cannot but pause and drop a tear at the thought that those who are brethren [the British and Americans], should be jealous of each other, and should be preparing for war as if common enemies."[56] He appears torn by the tensions between nostalgia for the soft imperialism of former times and a determination to resist political oppression.

If Heath's rationale for resistance was surprisingly inchoate, it surely drew energy from a tetchiness that had long historical roots, from a feeling of disrespect dating back to the founding of Massachusetts, and inflamed every time Britain either ignored New Englanders or legislated against their interests. The sense of not quite being fully English eased during times of prosperity. But it was always there. Although Heath lacked a well-formed political philosophy, he voiced at a moment of imperial crisis what might be called a New England legacy, a shared identity based on an imagined heritage. The enduring thread in this powerful narrative was an uncompromising love of liberty.[57] The point is not that the works of political theorists such as Locke did not matter to the community of which Heath was a part. They did. But when the region faced invasion, what really mattered was the blood of ancestors. In this environment, one word—liberty—could trigger an emotional response requiring no intellectual justification.

* * *

For soldiers on both sides of the conflict, the siege of Boston involved occasional alarms that seldom developed into major actions. Heath spent his days overseeing the fortification of Dorchester Heights, a responsibility he relished. He never encountered Burgoyne, who was scheming for greater glory. His pleading letters to London finally gave him the chance. The ministry allowed him to leave Massachusetts, and eager to share his plans for a major campaign from Canada to the Hudson Valley, he sailed on December 5, 1775. For the Americans, his departure was welcome news. One revolutionary informed John Adams, "It is with Confidence said that Burgoyne has not been seen in Action, and it is given out that he is gone Home. We are not without our Hopes that we shall have little trouble from his Enterprising Genius."[58] For his part, Burgoyne observed, "There is hardly a leading man among the rebels, in council or in the field, but at a proper time, and by proper management, might have been bought."[59]

Before departing, Burgoyne wrote a play, described either as a satire or a farce. The first performance of *The Blockade of Boston* occurred on January 9, 1776. Faneuil Hall—where, not long before, Americans had organized protests against British taxation—had been transformed into a stage. No text has survived, but people who had heard reports about Burgoyne's intentions anticipated that the leaders of the Continental Army would appear as simpletons. One person attended the theater expecting that Burgoyne would mock "the figures and manner of the Yankee soldiers, and by all accounts a very laughable thing."[60] The character playing George Washington ridiculed George Washington as a country bumpkin.

The curtain never went up. Just before the performance was scheduled to begin, a sergeant in full uniform appeared onstage. He warned the audience, composed mostly of British officers, that they should immediately return for duty. There was an emergency. Although his exact words are not known, the sergeant apparently exclaimed something to the effect that the Americans were coming. The warning made sense, since British intelligence had revealed that Washington wanted to launch a full-scale attack on Boston. But in the context of an evening's entertainment, no one took the warning seriously. Everyone assumed that the sergeant was a character in Burgoyne's play. It took some time before the officers were persuaded to leave Faneuil Hall. They quickly discovered that in fact the Americans were not coming. The incident that sparked the alarm turned out to be only an attack on several houses in Charlestown that British snipers used to harass American troops. One disappointed Boston loyalist noted that the rebels "certainly in this affair got the laugh against us."[61]

Or so it seemed. The American operation that set off a false alarm involved destroying eight houses in Charlestown without provoking a major firefight. Only one shot was fired, and that sound persuaded a larger contingent of British soldiers guarding Bunker Hill that Americans were attacking in full force. Over five hundred Continental soldiers were called into action. One was a promising young officer, David Henley. His bravery that night received special commendation from his superiors. Washington described Henley as "an active and Spirited Officer."[62] At that moment, no one could have foreseen that men whose lives were forever changed by the American Revolution—Burgoyne, Heath, and Henley—would soon clash in a Cambridge courtroom.

Mercy Otis Warren, New England's revolutionary playwright and historian, could not tolerate allowing Burgoyne to have the last word—at least, not in Boston. Soon after the false alarm interrupted his farce, a local company performed Warren's theatrical response, *The Blockheads: Or, The Affrighted Officers.* The work was ponderous, didactic, intended as an ideological comeback rather than as traditional entertainment. The play opens with a speech by a character named Puff, who laments the failure of the British army to defeat the Americans. He addressed a group of discouraged officers. Burgoyne is among them. "We came to America, flushed with high expectations of conquest, and curbing these sons of riot," declares Puff. "We toured away . . . as if our success was certain; as if we had only to curb a few licentious villains, or hang them as spectacles for their brethren."[63]

When he left Boston in December 1775, Burgoyne would have summarily rejected Puff's gloomy assessment. Victory over the Americans seemed inevitable. Burgoyne insisted he had it in his capacity to end the war quickly. All he needed were the military resources and personal authority he deserved. Burgoyne presented the king and the members of his cabinet with a bold plan outlined in "Reflections upon the War in America."[64] It explained how Burgoyne would lead an army down from Canada, cutting off New England from the other rebellious states. The proposed campaign generated a lot of enthusiasm in London. No one anticipated a humiliating defeat at Saratoga.

• CHAPTER 3 •

Encounters on the Road

Joyous news arrived in Boston on October 23, 1777. General Burgoyne had just surrendered over six thousand soldiers at Saratoga to the American General Horatio Gates. The stunning victory was especially timely, since with the exception of George Washington's surprising success at Trenton, the war had not gone well for the Americans. To be sure, the British had evacuated Massachusetts more than a year earlier, and the major revolutionary battles were now waged far from Massachusetts. But the fear and resentment remained.

Victory called for a huge celebration. The members of the state legislature declared the event a "remarkable appearance of Divine providence in favor of this and the United States." They called for a thanksgiving and special sermon by a leading minister. Thirteen cannons blasted away. Bonfires illuminated the night. A fast boat carried the glorious report to the American commissioners in Paris.[1] Abigail Adams marked the occasion with a spontaneous visit to Boston. She explained to John, "The joyful News of the Surrender of General Burgoyne and all his Army to our Victorious Troops prompted me to take a ride this afternoon with my daughter to Town to join tomorrow with my Friends in thanksgiving and praise to the Supreme Being who hath so remarkably delivered our Enemies into our Hands."[2] And in Cambridge, a more masculine observance occurred when "a number of principal gentlemen, both of the town and army, spent an agreeable evening in company, where many toasts were drank."[3] General Heath joined the festivities. His support for the American cause was as strong as ever, but his own military experience after the British abandoned Boston in 1776 had been disappointing. However many books he read about the military tactics of Frederick the Great, he seemed unable to translate theory into practice. After learning about a failed operation Heath had organized outside New York City, some American officers concluded that he was not suited to lead complex field operations.[4] Fortunately, Heath possessed other valuable talents, and Washington assigned Heath the command of Continental forces in New England. In this post he organized the purchase and transfer of military supplies and supervised the recruitment of soldiers. The duties were demanding. It helped that Heath was well-known and respected in the region, and under conditions that often strained his patience, he compiled a commendable record.

Heath soon discovered the victory at Saratoga had a major downside. In fact, Burgoyne's surrender presented him with an unprecedented set of problems for which he had no experience. The Continental Congress ordered him to establish a large prisoner-of-war camp, where Burgoyne's army would be housed until its status could be determined: Was he a prisoner of war or a parolee? Half of the soldiers did not speak English. Heath was responsible for providing lodging, securing guards, and, as winter approached, supplying firewood. In his *Memoirs,* he describes an almost panicky response to the challenge. Writing in the third person, he explained that "the capture of Gen. Burgoyne and his whole army, who were now on their way to Boston, opened a new, important and delicate field for our General."[5] The reference to an "important and delicate field" hugely understated Heath's challenge. Although he did not yet know it, he was about to confront Burgoyne in a contest over the meaning of independence.

Preparing a prison camp for so many men seemed an almost impossible task.[6] There was another concern, one that Heath shared with other revolutionaries. Many officers in Burgoyne's army came from England's ruling class. Several were members of Parliament. A few sat in the House of Lords. The presence of so many aristocrats posed a problem for Heath. After all, as he stated uneasily, "there were many officers of military erudition and some of refined and courtly manners, who had a high opinion of national honour and prowess."[7] How, he wondered, would these men respond to orders from an American general who not only supported independence but also was a farmer from Roxbury? In a new republican regime were these aristocrats still entitled to special deference? Cultural practices developed during long colonial rule could not easily be laid aside.

Heath's apprehensions about the consequences of Saratoga hardly compared with Burgoyne's gloom. After all, he had surrendered a large army, and he had done so after assuring the king and leading government ministers that his bold Canadian plan would hasten the end of the war. On almost every count, he failed. It is no wonder that William Pitt, a highly respected political figure in England, described the defeat as "that melancholy disaster."[8] And it was not surprising that Burgoyne blamed the situation on almost everyone else associated with the campaign: He never received expected supplies, the number of troops was less than he needed, the Native Americans proved unreliable allies, the roads through the forests of northern New York were impassable, and General William Howe, the British officer who was supposed to meet Burgoyne's army near Albany and thereby cut New England off from the other rebellious states, decided to take his troops from New York City south to Philadelphia, thus leaving Burgoyne exposed to an unexpectedly large American force.[9]

There was some truth in every charge, but the blame—at least, in England—fell squarely on Burgoyne. And he knew it. Throughout his negotiations with Heath, Burgoyne struggled to defend his reputation at home. With hindsight we can see that extraordinary hubris contributed hugely to his loss, but as many other overconfident military leaders have learned, another element contributed to Burgoyne's fall. As Sir Guy Carleton, the commander of British forces in Canada, wrote soon after the surrender, "This unfortunate event, it is to be hoped, will in future prevent ministers from pretending to direct operations of war in a country at 3,000 miles distance, of which they have so little knowledge as not to be able to distinguish between good, bad, or interested advices."[10]

Following the surrender and during the long march to Cambridge, Heath and Burgoyne experienced extreme personal stress, the result of fear, misinformation, and overconfidence. In Boston, Heath prepared for the flood of prisoners while Burgoyne tried to salvage his reputation. Among other things, the pressure of the moment meant that both men tended to express expectations and complaints in exaggerated language. They were keenly aware of the various audiences closely following their actions and words: prisoners of war, British political figures, civilians in New England, members of the Continental Congress, and, for Heath in particular, George Washington. As public figures, they assumed major roles in an unfolding drama. Burgoyne projected a shrewd awareness of theatrics, certainly more so than did Heath. But both men presented themselves during this period as slightly exaggerated representatives of competing cultures. Such behavior was to be expected—occurring frequently among leaders who have negotiated decolonization throughout the modern world—but in narratives of the American Revolution the phenomenon of self-conscious presentation is often overlooked.

* * *

John Trumbull shaped how many Americans today imagine the Revolution. A prolific artist, he captured the likenesses of the leading figures of the founding generation. He insisted on detail and accuracy. His *George Washington at Trenton* is a masterpiece, depicting

The Surrender of General Burgoyne at Saratoga, October 16, 1777, John Trumbull, ca. 1822–32. Oil on canvas, 21⅛ × 30⅝ × 1 in. (Yale University Art Gallery, Trumbull Collection)

the general's courage and determination in the face of battle. During the 1790s, Trumbull traveled widely throughout the new republic, making sketches of survivors of the Revolution. He later drew on these small drawings to complete massive historical paintings. Late in life—he died in 1843 at the age of eighty-seven—Trumbull accepted a commission from Congress for four huge canvasses now hanging in the Capitol Rotunda. One of them depicts a crucial turning point in 1777, the surrender of General Burgoyne at Saratoga, which led in February 1778 to the recognition of American independence by France.[11]

Trumbull rendered the central figures at the surrender so accurately that we can now identify not only Generals Gates and Burgoyne but also minor officers such as Generals Glover and Whipple, American officers who figured centrally in the winter journey to Cambridge. But however much the painter strove to capture an event he believed changed the course of history, he was a product of another era. He imagined Burgoyne's defeat through the lens of nineteenth-century nationalism. The canvas reflects a buoyant sense of America's special destiny. It was a belief amplified by the country's resistance to Great Britain during the War of 1812. This expansive vision of the nation's future added to the appeal of Trumbull's revolutionary art. Viewers to this day still interpret the *Surrender of General Burgoyne* from that perspective. Like many paintings of significant historical events, the work offers modern Americans a patriotic rendering of the Revolution almost a half century after Gates met Burgoyne at Saratoga. The huge flag flying over the tent communicates a widely accepted notion of "Manifest Destiny," an assumption that God intended Americans to rule the continent. The two generals—one American, one British—exchange swords, a ritual of honor, behavior one would expect in a civilized nation—or in one that wants to remember itself in that way.

To fault Trumbull for reimagining the country's origins from the patriotic perspective of the nineteenth century would be unfair. Drawing attention to elements he ignored at Saratoga certainly does not call into question his impressive artistic talent. But we might let our eye wander beyond a group of remarkably dapper military figures. Not far from the site of the formal surrender was an encampment of over six thousand soldiers who had served under Burgoyne's command. The exact number will never be known. Some were Canadians who fought for the king. British and German troops made up the largest group. There were also about 250 women, most of them wives who had followed husbands during the campaign. Dependent children numbered perhaps another five hundred.[12] At the moment Gates and Burgoyne exchanged swords—a ritual of surrender—these people were suffering both physically and psychologically. They were cold, wet, and very angry. Many had been moved to primitive field hospitals. They had witnessed the death of friends.

Regular British soldiers directed little criticism at Burgoyne—at least, no evidence of grumbling in the ranks has survived. The dominant emotion was embarrassment, since the defeat of such a formidable British force was an unprecedented failure. Roger Lamb, a British sergeant, tried to make the best of the situation, praising the courage of the British army in face of overwhelming American force. "It was consoling," he later observed in a memoir, "that we had preserved the dignity of the British character and extorted from a successful foe, vastly outnumbering us and straining every nerve to tarnish our honour, so plain an admission of the awe in which they held our enfeebled arms."[13]

The American force was in fact much larger, numbering at least fifteen thousand soldiers when Burgoyne surrendered. Some were Continentals, soldiers enlisted in the regular United States army. Daniel Morgan's riflemen traveled to Saratoga from as far away as Winchester, Virginia. But most of Gates's troops were militiamen, ordinary farmers for the most part who came from all parts of New England. Their numbers grew impressively during the last weeks of the campaign. Why they welcomed the chance to confront Burgoyne's army is difficult to gauge. Many may have wanted to defend the American cause; others may have responded to the prospect of adventure. A more compelling incentive to fight, however, probably sprang from a base emotion seldom seen as a component of revolutionary patriotism: the sting of imperial condescension, an awareness that in the eyes of their enemy they were not fully British but something lesser. Burgoyne managed to communicate profound disrespect for the Americans twice during his ill-fated expedition, and more than the lack of a coherent military strategy, his open disdain for his opponents contributed to his defeat.[14]

On June 20, 1777—several months before the surrender—Burgoyne issued a proclamation mocking the Americans' fight for independence. He may have thought the message a clever way to persuade those who still questioned separation from Great Britain to come forward and reaffirm allegiance to the king. He badly misread the situation. The statement had exactly the opposite impact on public opinion. It served to remind Americans that even as colonists—allegedly when they were still loyal subjects of the king—the British had not viewed them as fully English. Of course, Burgoyne's patronizing language drew upon a long history of imperialism. It was an ideology that took for granted British superiority and justified racist policies toward subject peoples. The sting of insult was especially obnoxious for New Englanders such as Heath who assumed they were the equals of the English men and women who happened to live in East Anglia or Kent.

Burgoyne failed to comprehend why the Americans would take offense. Oblivious to the situation on the ground, he appealed to loyalists—like so many generals in modern times, he assumed that the number was greater than it actually was—to realize that "the present unnatural Rebellion" has brought forth an arbitrary system of government that, among other things, offended God. Burgoyne's list of alleged rebel atrocities included "Arbitrary imprisonment, confiscation of property, persecution and torture, unprecedented in the inquisitions of the Romish Church." The comparison between the American enforcement of the Revolution and the trials of the Inquisition was particularly inept. During the Seven Years' War, New Englanders viewed the conflict in Canada in part as an attack on Catholicism—or, as they insisted, a crusade against the Antichrist. Hostility to the Romish Church had not abated since the end of that war.

Burgoyne maintained surrender was the only way for the Americans to avoid disaster. Indeed, if the rebels did not soon reaffirm their former allegiance, Burgoyne would be compelled to authorize "the Indian Forces under my direction, and they amount to Thousands, to overtake the harden'd Enemies of Great Britain . . . wherever they may lurk." American rebels could expect no mercy. Describing his army as divinely sanctioned, Burgoyne concluded: "The messengers of justice & wrath await them [revolutionaries] in the Field, and devastation, famine, and every concomitant horror that . . . prosecution of Military duty must occasion, will bar the way to their return." Such intemperate language has almost never persuaded people resisting what they regard as oppression to disperse and go home. In fact, extreme threats of retribution usually generate a renewed commitment to fight. And so, Burgoyne learned.[15]

The Native Americans in the British campaign raised another issue that might best be described as dueling racism. Although Burgoyne insisted he needed Native warriors, he thoroughly distrusted them. At best, he tolerated them—or so he claimed. The Native Americans recruited from different Northern tribes probably had only passing interest in restoring British rule, and as they made clear during several confrontations with Burgoyne, they viewed the conflict primarily as an opportunity to plunder Britain's enemies. When he tried to curtail their activities, the Native Americans threatened to desert. Maintaining a fragile alliance forced Burgoyne to let the warriors conduct warfare as they saw fit. In his eyes they were savages. As he later observed, "I had discerned the caprice, the superstition, the self-interestedness of the Indian character from the first intercourse, even with those nations which are supposed to have made the greatest progress towards civilization."[16]

Despite their alleged "ferocity," Burgoyne deployed the Native Americans against the revolutionaries. What else could he do? "I was convinced a cordial reconciliation with the Indians was only to be effected by a renunciation of all my former prohibitions and an indulgence in blood and rapine," he wrote.[17] The Americans shared Burgoyne's racism. How, they wondered, could the representative of a so-called civilized nation turn Native warriors against white colonists? Such a policy amounted to profound disrespect. Apparently, it did not matter that the revolutionaries also relied on Native Americans. Expediency always provided a convenient excuse.

Burgoyne's menacing pronouncements came to nothing. His elaborate plan to end the war was probably doomed from the start. He might have saved his army if he had retreated when that option was still a possibility. But he insisted through the summer of 1777 on marching toward Albany. A mixture of arrogance and stubbornness contributed to Burgoyne's final defeat. When it became obvious that the British no longer had the supplies or manpower to continue the fight, General Gates laid out the terms of surrender. To his surprise, Burgoyne rejected the proposal out of hand. Gates had not misread the situation. In his initial communication with Burgoyne, he declared, "General Burgoyne's Army being exceedingly reduced by repeated Defeats, by desertion, Sickness &c. their Provisions exhausted, their military Horses, Tents and Baggage taken or destroyed, their retreat cut off and their Camp invested, they can only be allowed to surrender Prisoners of War."[18] Burgoyne took umbrage at being classified as a prisoner of war. Such an offer was humiliating, an affront to the honor of British troops.

Burgoyne knew how to bluff. If he could not obtain the surrender he desired, he would continue to fight. For him, the sticking point was the American assumption that he and his soldiers were prisoners of war. Burgoyne warned that if Gates did not back down, "The Army will to a Man proceed to any Act of Desperation rather than submit to that Article."[19] It must have been obvious that Burgoyne was not prepared to make a hopeless last stand in the name of honor. But surprisingly, when Gates received Burgoyne's ultimatum, he yielded and opened a fresh round of negotiation.

The British general acted as if the negotiating parties were drawing up a formal treaty between sovereign nations. Burgoyne referred to the document as a "compact."[20] There was little precedent for such an agreement. In this strange situation, Gates and Burgoyne hammered out the articles of surrender. The text does in fact read like a contract. And that is why it will become so central to our story. The two generals at Saratoga may have thought that they had reached a clear understanding of the arrangement, but as with many legal statements, each detail invited interpretation. Burgoyne's clever defense of British honor would soon generate disputes about Heath's veracity, Henley's character, and the reputation of the United States among so-called civilized nations.

This unusual military agreement unexpectedly accelerated Americans along the road to cultural independence. Gates and Burgoyne signed the surrender document, the Convention of Saratoga, on October 16, 1777. It contained thirteen separate articles, some more significant than others. The first seemed straightforward. The British pledged "to march out of their camp with honours of war" and give up their artillery and other weapons. Officers, however, were permitted "to wear their side arms." Burgoyne's entire army received permission to journey directly to Boston, as fast as possible, from where the British assumed navy transports would carry them back to England. The only concession Burgoyne allowed to the Americans at Saratoga was that his soldiers would not serve "again in North America during the present contest." In other words, they could sail home, all six thousand, promising to remain there for as long as the war continued. No one hazarded an end date.[21]

Burgoyne's treaty also laid out precisely how the Americans would treat the defeated troops during the long trip from Saratoga to Boston. For him, retaining command was a matter of personal honor. After all, as he repeatedly insisted, they were not prisoners. They were only enemy soldiers passing freely through New England on parole. And as such, they were to receive the same "rations" as did Gates's men. The care and feeding of the British came at a cost, however, for so long as they were in the United States on parole, the British were obliged to pick up the bill. No one thought to stipulate how the accounts were to be settled—in gold, in pounds, or in Continental dollars.

The compact called for the Convention Army to take the most direct route to the Atlantic port. No unnecessary delays along the way would be tolerated, and in Burgoyne's mind, most important, during their entire stay in rebel territory, the Americans could exercise no direct authority over the British and German parolees. Military orders remained the prerogative of British officers. Cases of criminality, drunkenness, or disobedience wherever they occurred—along the road to Boston or in camp waiting for return to England—remained the sole responsibility of British officers. Burgoyne was adamant. He was the commander of the British force, and he not only issued orders but also demanded to be treated as what he was—a member of Parliament and a leading British officer. And as such, he demanded housing during his stay that reflected his social and military status. "Upon the march and during the time the Army shall remain in Quarters in Massachusetts Bay, the Officers are not as far as circumstances will admit to be separated from their men," he stated. "The officers are to be quartered according to rank, and are not to be hindered from assembling their men for roll call, and other necessary purposes of Regularity."[22]

Burgoyne apparently shared the contents of the Convention agreement with the regular British soldiers. It was a wise move. However humiliated they may have felt about the surrender, they departed Saratoga as parolees confident they would not be treated along the way as common prisoners of war. They could count on a military future stationed in England or Ireland. Hope—always an unreliable emotion—meant that during day-to-day interaction with the Americans, the British initially had little incentive to resist or complain. Boston was only a brief stopping place on the trip home. One German solider carefully listed in a private letter all the conditions that defined the Convention Army. The only difference in his notes from the official compact was the expectation that the surrender of arms would be accompanied "with bands playing."[23] A nice touch. Not exactly a festive occasion, but the music steadied the nerves. At that moment it must have seemed as if Burgoyne had managed to lessen the sting of defeat.

The obvious question—then and now—is why Gates accepted Burgoyne's extraordinary demands. After all, the Americans controlled the battlefield. He received praise from members of the Continental Congress. Eliphalet Dyer, a delegate from Connecticut, viewed Gates as the special agent of the Lord: "He hath made you the happy instrument in bringing down the lofty pride and haughty insolence of a Vain glorious Burgoyne, who has spread terror and Consternation through our Northern County."[24]

One plausible explanation of Gates's behavior, accepted by many people at the time, was that he had received alarming military intelligence that General Henry Clinton was moving north from the

British base in New York City with orders to relieve Burgoyne. It was a case of too little too late. Clinton did not have sufficient troop strength seriously to threaten the Americans. Philipp Waldeck, a German then serving in the British army, described the futility of a possible rescue: "It reminds me of when the doctor goes to visit a sick patient who died the day before."[25]

Others suspected that Gates, who until recently had been an officer in the British army, was overly solicitous in demonstrating proper respect to his old colleague Burgoyne. He subscribed to a code of honor held dear by British gentlemen. John Andrews, an eighteenth-century British historian, explained such behavior: "Sentiments of generosity [were not] wanting in the American general. Being himself a native of Britain, it is not improbable that, though engaged in the cause of America, he still retained those feelings for the reputation of his country; of which it has long been observed, that military men, more than all others, are never willing to divest themselves, though in arms against it."[26] Another possible reason for Gates's curious decisions is hard to document. We know that he was inordinately ambitious—a character flaw that frequently put him at odds during the war with Washington—and he may have wanted to claim the full glory for Saratoga before his American rival who was resisting a British army near Philadelphia could object.[27]

If that was in fact Gates's reasoning, he was badly mistaken. John Rutledge, a leading member of the Continental Congress from South Carolina, was willing to give Gates the benefit of doubt, but he made it clear that "I dislike the terms of the Convention much."[28] Abigail Adams also tried to put a good face on Burgoyne's treaty. She reported to John Adams, "I have read many Articles of Capitulation, but none which ever contained so generous Terms before. Many people find fault with them but perhaps do not consider sufficiently the circumstances of General Gates, who [perhaps] by delaying and exacting more might have lost all."[29] The Reverend Samuel Cooper, a highly respected Congregational minister in Boston who was offered the presidency of Harvard, informed John

Adams, "In my present Opinion, Infatuation or something worse, dictated the Concessions made to an Army, not a third of ours in Number."[30] Throughout Massachusetts, tales of the strange surrender encouraged skeptical rumors, if not outright fears of conspiracy.

Drawing on his judgment of character—he did not trust Burgoyne—and common sense, Washington declared that he smelled a rat. Pointing out the obvious, he explained to fellow Virginian Richard Henry Lee that it was entirely possible Burgoyne's army would return to England only to be replaced immediately by an equal number of British troops. If that was the plan, then the Convention would achieve nothing to help the Americans win the war. "I think this will happen," he wrote from the battle front in Pennsylvania, "and unless great delicacy is used in the precautions . . . they will justify, a breach of the Covenant on their part." Washington was certain that the British would justify their trickery on the grounds that "no faith is to be held with Rebels."[31]

No evidence survives indicating that Burgoyne contemplated such a deceitful scheme—at least, not at that moment. He may have had his mind on other things. His travails certainly did not discourage him from partying with his mistress, the wife of a member of his staff, or later relaxing over a good meal and drink at the home of a wealthy American, Major General Philip Schuyler, whose manor house had recently been destroyed by the British army. The Baroness von Riedesel, who was married to the commander of the German forces, noted in her journal that Burgoyne "liked having a jolly time and spending half the night singing and drinking and amusing himself in the company of the wife of a commissary, who was his mistress and, like him, loved champagne."[32] Burgoyne may have assumed that since he had bested Gates during the surrender negotiations, he could openly indulge in pleasures befitting aristocratic status.

Burgoyne's immediate concern centered on real and imagined political enemies in England. As he had done throughout his career, he blamed other people for the defeat at Saratoga. In one of his few personal letters to have survived, he informed his nieces, "I have been surrounded with enemies, ill-treated by pretended friends, abandoned by a considerable part of my own army, totally unassisted by Sir William Howe." He had endured martyrdom in America for a noble cause: "I have been with my army within the jaws of famine; shot through my hat and waistcoat; my nearest friends killed around me; and after these combined misfortunes and escapes, I imagine I am reserved to stand a war with ministers who will always lay the blame upon the employed who miscarries."[33] As he knew full well from his political experience in Parliament, his dramatic description of self-sacrifice would soon circulate in London, becoming a public explanation as to why he was not responsible for failure.

For the ordinary troops the ritual of formal surrender passed without incident. The British soldiers filed down to the bank of the Hudson River and, according to the Convention, peacefully stacked their weapons. As might be expected, there was a lot of grumbling about a defeat that most of them thought should not have occurred. The English troops were not, as some have imagined, men who served in the army out of desperation. Although they came largely from the lower class, they were not criminals. Most joined the military for economic reasons, a decision that involved a commitment of many years. The army became a career lasting until they were pensioned off. It is not surprising that wives of some soldiers followed their husbands, and of course, experienced the same hardships, rain, cold, and disease. The only substantial difference between the English troops and the Germans was that the Germans were hired to fight.[34] They seem to have defined their service less out of an ideological commitment to defend the British empire than from a sense of loyalty to a powerful Hanoverian aristocrat who recruited them and paid their wages.

The American soldiers who witnessed the final surrender of weapons stood silently. They, too, were wet and cold. And proud as well. Musicians played "Yankee Doodle." Although no one at the time could have predicted that the Revolution would last for six more years, Gates's troops gained a measure of confidence in their own abilities to hold their own against the British. Charles Stedman, a loyalist and officer in the British army, believed the victory at Saratoga gave the Americans "fresh ardour . . . [and] lessened in the mind of the American soldier the high opinion which he had entertained of British valour and discipline, and inspired him with a juster confidence of himself."[35]

A German soldier described the final scene from a different perspective. For him, the Americans challenged how ordinary troops were supposed to look. By European standards, they did not seem professional. He expected matching uniforms. But on a chilly October day, the Americans who filed down to the surrender field appeared in "the clothes in which he goes to the field, to church, or to the tavern." More curious still, during an intensely emotional moment, these citizen soldiers "stood so still that we were greatly amazed. Not one fellow made a motion as if to speak to his neighbor." The compliment raises questions. What sort of behavior had the German anticipated? Did he think the Americans would reveal themselves as undisciplined rabble incapable of honor and respect? He did not hazard an answer, but he had to admit that these Americans were unlike any other soldiers the German had ever encountered. The victors were "so slender, so handsome, so sinewy, that it was a pleasure to look at them." Whatever the cause that had brought them to Saratoga, there could be no doubt that America "excels most of Europe in respect to the stature and beauty of its men."[36]

* * *

By late October 1777, the bright color of fall leaves had given way to a dreary transitional season. The days were cold, often damp, and without a snow cover, travel became tedious, nearly impossible in places. The roads connecting small villages turned to mud. On October 17, the entire Convention Army set off from Saratoga to Cambridge, a journey of some two hundred miles. Burgoyne's soldiers may have thought they were slogging their way to Boston, to British transports that would carry them back to England. But the plans changed. The destination was Cambridge, nearby but safely away from wharves where enemy ships might dock.

For these people—regular soldiers, women, and children—the challenge of surviving the mud and cold was especially daunting. One woman gave birth in the open air. She survived. Several soldiers died of exposure. The senior officers engaged lodging in private homes, but the others found shelter as best they could, usually in barns. One British solider recounted the chaos: "It is impossible to describe the confusion . . . carts breaking down, others sticking fast, some oversetting, horses tumbling with their loads of baggage, men cursing, women shrieking, and children squalling."[37]

For all the suffering that the journey from Saratoga involved, it offered an unusual opportunity for adversaries to take a measure of each other without the fear of violence. Americans living in the small villages of Massachusetts had not previously encountered enemy troops. Of course, they had followed the events in Boston that culminated in the military occupation of the city. However, the war had only indirectly touched the countryside. The face of the Revolution were local committees of safety and observation made up of neighbors. Burgoyne's surrender brought the war home, turning imagined foes into real people. Encounters occurred dramatically on scattered farms and town greens, as thousands of German and British soldiers interrupted daily routines. The exchanges along the road—chance conversations, expressions of curiosity, and slagging remarks—alerted Americans to cultural differences. The same conditions confronted the soldiers of the Convention Army. During a long campaign, they had formed opinions of American troops, but now, on the journey to Cambridge, they formed personal impressions of the ordinary civilians who had so recently rejected the empire. They were not anthropologists, of course, but as a British sergeant observed, "On this march we were able to make comparisons between the appearance and manner of life of the inhabitants and our own people at home."[38]

During the march to Cambridge, the Americans separated the Germans from the British soldiers. The decision reflected what had been normal practice in the British army. Truth be told, Burgoyne did not much like the Germans, and in an extremely undiplomatic outburst, he suggested that the entire expedition from Canada might have gone better if he had had more British and fewer German troops, a remark that greatly irritated Major General Riedesel.[39] The Germans traveled a southern route to Springfield; the British passed through Williamstown and Northampton.

The American officer assigned overall command of the transfer of the prisoners—they insisted they were parolees—was General John Glover, among whose other accomplishments during the Revolution was the creation of the first fully integrated regiment and, during the winter of 1776, the organization of a flotilla of boats that carried Washington to a much-needed victory at Trenton. A tough merchant and fisherman, he thoroughly disliked escorting the British to Cambridge. Since Burgoyne agreed to pay for his army's expenses while they remained in the United States, Glover had to gather receipts from farmers along the route who claimed the loss of an animal or destruction of a fence. He suspected that many alleged charges were exaggerated, perhaps even fraudulent, but many weeks after Burgoyne had arrived in Cambridge, Glover was still collecting pieces of paper. The American guards were local militiamen who received a penny per mile for their service.[40]

Glover was ably assisted by General William Whipple Jr., who before the war had been a merchant in New Hampshire. He was involved in the trade of enslaved people, something that would undoubtedly merit condemnation today. But there is good evidence that the experience of revolution, especially the rhetoric of rights and equality, transformed how Whipple viewed his former life. He later freed Prince Whipple, an enslaved person, but at the time he wrote, "A recommendation is gone thither for raising some regiments of Blacks. This, I suppose will lay the foundation for the emancipation of those wretches. . . . I hope it will be the means of dispensing the blessings of Freedom to all the human race in

America." Hannah Winthrop liked to tell how Whipple bested a British general who asked during the march to Cambridge why anyone had ever bothered to cross "the Atlantic & go through such difficulty to conquer so unfavorable a Country which would not be worth keeping when conquered." When the British prisoners "came to the banks of the Connecticut river, General Whipple said to him this is the country which we are fighting for. Ah, replied the [British] general, this is a country worth a ten years war."[41]

The Germans seem to have been genuinely curious about the United States. To be sure, there were unpleasant moments. Local farmers complained about theft, something not all that surprising considering the bad weather and limited rations. In response, the Germans accused the Americans of stealing horses. To which the locals "tell us that we have either stolen them ourselves, or else have bought them from persons friendly to the King, who in turn have stolen the horses from them [revolutionary farmers]!"[42]

Senior officers who owed their military positions to aristocratic favor in Germany viewed the Americans they encountered with disdain. Perhaps they suspected that the assumption of social equality—at least among white Americans—might represent a looming threat to a privileged European order. Which, of course, it did. General Riedesel minced no words: "They [the Americans] are extremely inquisitive, credulous and zealous to madness for liberty."[43] Captain Cleve recorded an early example of political correctness, observing that the Americans "whom for politeness' sake we no longer call Rebels or *Jenkeys,* often do not know themselves to what category of people we really belong." Indeed, they kept asking the Germans what they did for a living when they were not soldiers. "Since the guards here are militia regiments," Cleve explained, "and almost all officers in them are manual laborers, it has cost us much trouble to impart the idea that our officers had no handicrafts."[44] The idea that men could spend their whole adult lives as professional soldiers struck the New England farmers as bizarre. A citizen was expected to follow a trade. Even more insulting, the

Americans rejected the notion that nobles deserved respect simply because they were nobles.

German soldiers who were not members of the ruling class in Brunswick or Hesse viewed the American social landscape from a different perspective. They were taken by the women they encountered, noting that they seemed in better physical condition than their European counterparts. According to the Germans, the explanation could be traced to the willingness of the women to undergo "inoculation against smallpox." The result of good medical practice was clearly evident in the communities along the road. "I have seen few [women] disfigured by pock-marks," one soldier reported.[45] The presence of so many enemy troops did not trigger fear. Instead of hiding in safe places, young women came out to see the strangers. One German observed, "At all places through which we passed, dozens of girls were met with on the road, who either laughed at us mockingly, or now and then roguishly offered us an apple, accompanied by a little curtsey."[46] During the war many German soldiers—in the Middle States especially—elected to stay in the United States, where rich farmland promised a better life than they could anticipate back home. There is no evidence, however, that these particular German prisoners succumbed to the playful flirtations of American Eves.

The Germans took a surprising interest in the impressive prosperity of the enslaved African Americans they encountered during the long march to Cambridge. One soldier's observations were predictably racist. He did not condemn slavery. In fact, he regarded enslaved people as little more than "cattle." Whatever his biases may have been, he discovered that almost every farm on the road to Springfield seemed to own an unfree Black family. What was most unexpected was the visible well-being of Black men and women. The labor that owners demanded was not too exhausting. In fact, "The Negro is looked upon in light of a servant to the farmer." Perhaps thinking in terms of the grinding poverty of peasant life in Germany, the letter writer concluded, "Take it all in all, slavery is not so bad."[47]

One might ask for whom was slavery not so bad? One German prisoner discovered that New Englanders sent enslaved persons "to war" in place of young white men trying to avoid military service. In fact, this racist practice explained—at least, for the German commentator—why "there is scarcely a regiment in which you shall not find some well-built and hardy [Black] fellows." Even more astonishing, free African Americans lived as well as their white neighbors. The observer claimed, "Many families of free Negroes are also met with here who reside in good houses, are in comfortable circumstances, and live as well as their white neighbors."[48]

Probably not. The German drew upon his own culture when drawing such conclusions. For all his inquisitiveness, the prisoner failed to understand that the enslaved men and women he encountered longed for freedom, for independence, an aspiration that many whites understood as well, for it was in this same region of Massachusetts that unfree Blacks first appealed successfully for the first time to state courts for liberty. He certainly failed to interview determined African American women such as Mumbet, later Elizabeth Freeman, who lived in Sheffield, west of Springfield. She would have explained she could not endure a life that did not include freedom. As she stated, "Any time, any time while I was a slave, if one minute's freedom had been offered to me, and I had been told I must die at the end of that minute, I would have taken it—just to stand one minute on God's *airth* a free woman—I would."[49]

Encounters on the journey to Cambridge only confirmed the opinions that the English prisoners had of the Americans. The soldiers may have been as curious about the local farmers as were the Germans, but the stories they recorded were almost always negative. The Americans remained former colonials who defied intelligent understanding by rejecting the British Empire. As rogue subjects, they would regret rebellion once the British regrouped and won the war. In British eyes, the people whose prosperity impressed the Germans were reduced to "peasants."[50] The word itself is significant in this context. The British soldiers would not have described even the poorest agricultural workers in England as peasants—perhaps in derogatory language, but not as peasants. Its use during the long march amounted to an insult, testimony that the colonists were second-class subjects, different and inferior to people who lived in England. Being called peasants surely annoyed the Americans who lined the road to watch a passing army.

British troops speculated about the root causes of rebellion. The most plausible explanation was that the Americans had succumbed to a kind of madness. Their irrational behavior revealed a lack of emotional self-control. Their ideas about independence had become impervious to argument. One soldier reported that even though the war had deprived the Americans of "the conveniences of life"—British household goods—they were still determined "to obtain that idle, *independency.*" In fact, the revolutionaries had transformed a rebellion into "a religious cause." The commentator knew exactly who was responsible for this unhappy state of affairs. It was the clergy. The British soldier insisted that a minister "in my hearing, firmly asserted, that rewards were prepared in Heaven for those who fell in the present contest." These claims served "to delude the ignorant." And the results were dangerous. This clergyman, "after pretending that he had been visited by the Supreme Being in visions," assured the people that "those only would be accepted in Heaven who should seal their lives in so religious a cause with their blood." A spirit of independence had poisoned the Americans. It even affected settlement patterns. According to the British, they insisted on distancing themselves from other people, "as if each family wished to assert its independence of neighbours and form a village consisting of its own house and barn."[51]

Other encounters had a more ambiguous quality. The British told each other stories about unsophisticated Americans who blended superstition and ignorance and who were therefore easy targets for more worldly soldiers. One humorous exchange occurred in Worcester, a town that had a long history of resistance to imperial rule. Sergeant Lamb observed that since the Americans were so curious—in fact, "the most inquisitive people in the world"—the British could not resist trying to discover how much they could bait the locals. During one incident, a Lieutenant M'Neil was settling into a room at an inn. The Americans would not leave him alone. They kept asking questions. He was especially annoyed by "the giggles and ironical curtsies of a row of very handsome young women who came out to see us at Worcester." One woman standing behind the others caught M'Neil's eye. This "small queer great-grand-mother in a tall hat . . . raised her Hands to Heaven and stared at us with astonishment." M'Neil had a ready riposte for such rude behavior. '"So, Mother Goose," he said, "must you come wandering out to see the lions?"' Not to be bested, she replied, "Lions, lions! I declare now I had mistook you for lambs." It is significant that a woman confronted the British traveler. She may have diffused a tense situation. A man who attempted to outwit a British sergeant would have risked sparking a physical confrontation. But when dealing with a group of British officers that included "no fewer than six members of Parliament and a number of peers," Old Mother Goose voiced a revolutionary community's rejection of aristocratic privilege.[52]

Lord Napier, a young lieutenant in Burgoyne's army and Scottish nobleman, had a similar, although much more bizarre experience in Worcester. Like M'Neil, he was "much troubled by the curiosity of the women at the house where he was lodged." They insisted that anyone called a lord must possess special attributes associated with divinity. Perhaps Napier must, in fact, be more than a normal man. And to settle the matter, the women "kept peeping in at doors and windows, in the hope of seeing a creature with angel's wings or devil's hoof and tail, or I know not what else." The female delegation would not be denied. They pushed into the room, where they challenged another lieutenant who attempted to preserve Napier's privacy. "We hear you have got a Lord among you," declared one female intruder. "Pray now, which may he be?" She warned the soldier, "Dare to deceive us and it will be worse for you." Napier, who had just fallen on a muddy road and had not cleaned up, suddenly presented himself. His fellow officer introduced him with impressive gravity: "Ladies, there you behold the form and person of the Right Honourable Francis Napier, of His Majesty's Thirty-first Regiment of Foot, Baron of Merchiston in the Kingdom of Scotland, Baronet of Novia Scotia, Hereditary Lord Almoner to the Akhood of Swat, Grand Squire of Gotham, Lord of hundred inferior lordships in the Land of Cockaigne, Knight Grand Cross of the Order of Liliburlero, and much besides which I have forgot." The women stared at the dirty Napier. Finally, one of them concluded, "Well, for my part, if *that* be a Lord, I never desire to see any other Lord than the Lord Jehovah."[53] It is difficult to tell who was pulling whose leg. The women who had been raised in a colonial regime knew full well that a British aristocrat was not a religious figure. And although the British may have had fun telling the story about these witless Americans, one suspects that in Worcester they were the ones who were the butt of the joke.

* * *

The dreary weather reflected the sullen mood of everyone involved. On November 7, 1777, Burgoyne's army arrived in Cambridge, soaking wet from a persistent cold rain.[54] The Convention Army entered in two separate groups—the Germans first and then, the next day, Burgoyne and the British regulars. His troops tried to project a sense of sangfroid. After all, they were not only scheduled to return to England, but they also remained confident that Great Britain would win the war.

The people who lived in Cambridge were not sure what to make of the spectacle. Six thousand enemy prisoners threatened to disrupt community life. Fortunately, a remarkable letter describing the tensions of the moment has survived. Hannah Winthrop was married to a distinguished Harvard professor, John Winthrop, a respected scholar who traced his family back to the founding of Massachusetts Bay in 1630. Hannah participated in his scientific

Hannah Winthrop, by John Singleton Copley, 1773. Oil on canvas, 35½ × 28¾. (The Metropolitan Museum of Art, New York, Morris K. Jesup Fund, 1931)

research. She also provided astute commentary on daily life in a revolutionary society. About her politics there is no doubt. Several years before the Americans declared independence, Hannah proclaimed that she—like other outspoken women of her generation—was prepared to support fully resistance to imperial rule. In 1774 she informed her friend Mercy Otis Warren, "be it known unto Britain, even American daughters are Politicians & Patriots and will aid the good work with their Female Efforts."[55]

The arrival of Burgoyne's army raised hard questions for Hannah about etiquette. Should she even give the intruders the time of day? Why not stay home and ignore the prisoners? Some neighbors counseled Americans to receive the strangers—especially those of high social standing in England—with proper respect. "Some polite ones," she noted, "say we ought not look on them as prisoners—that they are persons of distinguished rank. Perhaps, too, we must not view them in the light of enemies." Hannah thought such reasoning fatuous. In wartime, she wrote, the distinction between privileged status and enemy of the new republic "will soon be lost."[56]

Whatever her reservations about watching a defeated army in the rain, Hannah could not resist. She seems to have expected more than the bedraggled parade could offer. Memories of the rituals of colonial rule had not faded with independence. But the reality of what she witnessed on the road to Cambridge from Watertown was as surprising as it was depressing. She confessed, "We thought we should have nothing to do but view them as they passed. I never had the least idea that the Creation produced such a Sordid Set of Creatures in human Figure."[57]

The defenders of the British Empire turned out to be "poor, dirty, emaciated men." And they were accompanied by women "who seemed to be the beasts of burden, heavy bushel-baskets on their backs, by which they were bent double." There were wagons filled with pots and pans, and all sorts of furniture. Adding to this chaotic scene were children, even infants "who were born on the road." The sight of so many desperate women—"barefoot, clothed in dirty rags"—repelled Hannah. As did the smell. "Such Effusia filled the air while they were passing, had they not been smoaking all the time, I should have been apprehensive of being Contaminated by them." No wonder she was so concerned about the negative impact of these people on the town. The British brought fear back to Cambridge. Winthrop confessed, "I never thought I could lie down to sleep Surrounded by these enemies."[58]

Burgoyne took no notice of local distress. He entered the town accompanied by "a noble Looking advanced Guard." At that moment he seemed to embody imperial arrogance. The contrast with the American troops was unmistakable. These men represented the aspirations of a newly independent nation. Following the British soldiers into Cambridge were a "fine, Noble looking Guard of

American Brawny Victorious Yeomanry, who assisted in bringing these Sons of Slavery to Terms. Some of our Wagons drawn by fat oxen, driven by joyous looking Yankees."[59]

The Germans were assigned to Winter Hill; the British to Prospect Hill. The prisoners were in for a long winter. Captain Cleve of a Brunswick battalion feared for the worst: "The barracks have been erected without foundations, and with bare boards, through which, from above, below, and all around, drive in the wind, the rain, and the snow. They have no windows, only holes."[60] Despite such inadequate lodging, the Germans did not pose a serious problem for the American guards. It was the British assigned to Prospect Hill who could not tolerate being treated by the rebels as equals. Camp rules prohibited them from entering Boston. They often looked longingly down on the city from Prospect Hill, imagining impending liberation, passing the hours, much as Washington's troops had done more than a year earlier when the British occupied Boston. For the British, the ordeal had just begun.

• CHAPTER 4 •

Living with the Enemy

General Heath expected the first meeting with Burgoyne might not go well. He dreaded the moment. However, there was no getting around introducing the leading British officers to their American counterparts. Whatever his reservations, Heath felt it was his duty to treat his distinguished guests with proper respect, even though a polite reception could not hide the fact that the guests happened to be his prisoners. Heath knew that a lot could go wrong very quickly. Nevertheless, he wanted to demonstrate that a newly independent nation was also an honorable one. The dinner was just a start. With luck, he thought, the two groups could maintain civil relations until the Convention Army sailed home.

As the moment approached, the awkwardness of the situation became more apparent. Heath's headquarters were in Boston. Burgoyne and other British generals rode from Cambridge on impressive horses. It was a grand show. One might not have known that they had recently surrendered an entire army. Two major generals accompanied Burgoyne: Friedrich Riedesel, commander of the German forces, and William Phillips, a British officer who seems to have disliked Americans even more than did Burgoyne. Among the guests Heath invited were Generals Glover and Whipple, Continental officers who oversaw the long march from Saratoga. Heath reported that "an elegant dinner was prepared." He did not explain how these people managed to maintain a flow of polite conversation.

One topic loomed over the dinner party like a dark cloud. No one present was certain exactly how the articles of the so-called treaty signed by Gates would be implemented while the Convention Army remained in Massachusetts. The immediate question was the extent of Heath's authority over the British and German soldiers. What if one of them committed a crime on Prospect Hill? Could Heath mete out an appropriate punishment? That the issue was even in doubt was annoying. After all, Heath was in charge of American military affairs in what was called the Eastern Department. Nevertheless, Burgoyne was no ordinary prisoner of war. He was an English aristocrat, a member of Parliament, and, by his own light, a celebrity. The tension at dinner centered on whether a person of Burgoyne's social standing would take orders from an ordinary American.

General Phillips broached the delicate topic. Turning directly to Heath, he said, "Sir, you know well the disposition of soldiers, and that they will more or less in all armies commit some disorders." That being the case, Phillips suggested that Heath might want to "delegate to Gen. Burgoyne the power of seeing your orders executed." The American tried to deflect the implied challenge. Heath explained that he was fully aware of the need to preserve "order and obedience" among the prisoners. And he assumed Burgoyne possessed considerable discretionary power "as might appear to be necessary." However, there could be no mistake. Cooperation with the British did not compromise Heath's authority. Focusing his attention directly on Phillips, he declared, "as to the exercise of his own command, and enforcement of his own orders when necessary, this was a jurisdiction which Gen. Burgoyne must not expect to exercise while here." Burgoyne listened intently to the exchange. When he heard Heath's response, he offered only a smile. Phillips tried to make light of the situation, noting, "I only meant it for your easement, Sir." They all knew it was a warning shot.

After dinner Burgoyne suggested that the group take a walk through the center of town. Boston had not recovered from the British occupation. Mild weather probably encouraged a spontaneous excursion. The bizarre parade presented an unusual public spectacle. Even before the officers left the building where the generals dined, a large number of Americans gathered to see the man who had just surrendered an entire army. Hannah Winthrop was there. She claimed that Burgoyne drew "as great a number of spectators as ever attended a pope." The huge turnout caught Heath by surprise. "Before dinner was done," he reported, "so great was the curiosity of the citizens of both sexes, and of all ages and descriptions, to get a peep at Gen. Burgoyne, that the streets were filled, the doors, windows, the tops of the houses and fences crowded." He also noted that the people behaved themselves, perhaps better than he expected. He heard "not a word or a gesture that was disrespectful."

Not far from Boston Common, Burgoyne suddenly stopped. He wanted the American and British officers to take special note of an imposing structure known as Province House. In a loud voice, Burgoyne announced, "There is the former residence of the Governor."[1] The point of his pronouncement was not difficult to understand—especially for the Americans. For much of the eighteenth century, Province House had served as the center of British colonial government. Its very size expressed political power. Constructed originally in 1679, this three-story building of Jacobean style provided a magnificent setting for the royal governors of Massachusetts—all appointed by the king—to hold formal meetings as well as special social events. No one entering Province House could possibly have missed how every architectural detail projected imperial authority. A large, beautifully carved rendering of the royal coat of arms that hung over the massive front door served as a reminder of the former regime.[2]

Long after the Revolution, the building fell on hard times, but early in the nineteenth century its extraordinary symbolic history caught the imagination of Nathaniel Hawthorne. In "Legends of the

Province-House"—a story included in his *Twice-Told Tales*—he recounted entering a room where "the ancient governors held their levees, with vice-regal pomp, surrounded by the military men, the councillors, the judges, and other officers of the crown, while all the loyalty of the province thronged to do them honor." Hawthorne was happy that a new republican culture had emerged, freed from aristocratic pomp. Burgoyne had a very different perspective. At this moment, standing on a street in Boston, the outcome of the war still in doubt, he seemed to suggest that Province House and all that it once represented might yet be restored.

Just then, someone in the crowd interrupted Burgoyne's reflections on the old regime. According to Heath, the person, who was not identified—"in a tone fully to be heard"—exclaimed, "On the other side [of the street] is the riding school," a clear reference to Burgoyne's defacement of the Old South Church during the fall of 1775. Heath froze. Was the crowd about to attack the British general and his staff? Would angry Americans dishonor the new republic? Burgoyne pretended not to hear the complaint. And to Heath's immense relief, nothing happened. No one said another word. A few minutes later Burgoyne informed the American general, "Sir, I am astonished at the civility of your people; for were you walking the streets of London in my situation, you would not escape insult." The comment sounds like a compliment—somewhat backhanded, to be sure—but his observation could be interpreted to mean that the ordinary citizens of Boston were more civilized than he had expected. Or, he could have been reminding Heath that a rebel leader might one day face a hostile London mob.

The group of officers continued to where the ferry to Charlestown docked. Again, the people following Burgoyne said not a word. Heath was overjoyed. "O my dear countrymen," he confessed in his memoirs, "How did this your dignified conduct at the moment charm my very soul! Such conduct flows from a greatness of mind, that goes to conquer a world." The Yankees had passed the first test.[3]

* * *

Over the next several weeks, Heath managed to remain calm. One could certainly have understood if he had experienced moments of panic. He was responsible for providing food, fuel, and housing for over six thousand prisoners of war—a challenge he gamely described as "no small task."[4] Although he did not mention dependent women and children in his dispatches, Heath knew that he had to act quickly to minimize the human suffering on Prospect and Winter Hills. The weather did not cooperate. At the time, people complained of an unusually "piercing winter."[5]

And, of course, Heath had to provide a sufficient number of guards. He estimated that he would need between 1,000 and 1,200 American soldiers to secure the barracks.[6] To add to his burden, Heath was forced to negotiate every detail pertaining to supplies, housing, and behavior with different American groups who were generous with advice but short on resources. He often turned to Washington. The Continental Congress offered little more than encouragement, while the representatives of the Massachusetts government seemed determined to avoid taking fiscal responsibility for maintaining Burgoyne's army.

Confronted with these competing interests, Heath affirmed in an official release his determination "on the one hand to treat them [the prisoners] with politeness & humanity, and on the other with precaution and strict Order." Perhaps because he was uncertain how Burgoyne's soldiers would actually behave, Heath laid down basic rules of conduct. It was a prudent move, of course, but Heath lacked reliable precedent for controlling soldiers who, according to Burgoyne, were not technically prisoners of war. Among other things, the rules established a 9:00 p.m. curfew for regular soldiers, penalties for any British officers who exceeded the limits of parole, guidelines for the flow of provisions into the camps, including liquor, and the freedom of "the servants belonging to the officers who are on parole," who were advised "not to stroll from their master's quarters." The announcement also reported that the British had made a "promise" to stay within the "proscribed boundaries" of Prospect and Winter Hills, and more significantly, they had pledged to "not directly nor indirectly give any intelligence whatsoever to the enemies of the United States, or do or say anything in opposition to, or in prejudice of, the measures and proceedings of any Congress for the said States during [their] continuance."[7] One can imagine that after reading these regulations, American guards might have mumbled, "good luck with that."

For residents of Cambridge, living in close proximity to so many hostile strangers did little to inspire politeness and humanity. Before the war, they had welcomed American resistance to British taxation. Once protest turned to violence, however, they paid a heavy price. During the siege of Boston, George Washington selected Cambridge for his headquarters. Thousands of American soldiers flooded into the community. Barracks were thrown up overnight, most of them flimsy and, when the Convention Army arrived, in extreme disrepair. Harvard College had a long history in the town, but it too had suffered during the conflict.[8]

Even before Americans seriously considered independence, Cambridge drew a number of elite families from Boston who built impressive second homes. Many sympathized with imperial rule, and after the British abandoned Massachusetts, they fled, leaving behind a group of stately mansions that became known as Tory Row. Ann Hulton, a Boston loyalist, informed a friend: "There's a little genteel Town about 4 miles off called Cambridge, where a number of Gentlemen's Familys live upon their Estates." She dismissed Harvard with contempt: "Here is a Colledge indeed, but the independency and Liberty with which the Youths are brought up, makes too many of 'em proficient in Vice."[9] About the farmers who comprised most of the local population, she had nothing to say.

It is not surprising that the British prisoners expressed disappointment upon arriving in Cambridge. A sergeant in Burgoyne's army reported "there are a number of fine houses in [the community] going to decay, belonging to the Loyalists. The town must have been extremely pleasant, but its beauty is much defaced, being now only an arsenal for military stores."[10] He never adjusted to the harsh demands of incarceration and often rushed to the highest point on Prospect Hill, looking down on Boston Harbor just six miles away in hope of spotting a fleet of British transports that would take him back to England. They never came. Hannah Winthrop shared the sergeant's depression. She was not sure who to blame for the situation, but in a poignant letter to Mercy Otis Warren, she asked, "Is there not a degree of unkindness in loading poor Cambridge, almost ruined before this great army seemed to be let loose upon us? What will be the consequences, time will discover. . . . It is said we shall have not less than seven thousand persons to feed in Cambridge and its environs, more than its inhabitants."[11]

Without a doubt, the Convention Army contributed to the sour mood of a community that had recently backed resistance to Great Britain. What is also true is that the presence of so many hostile visitors amplified, but did not in itself cause, a growing sense of malaise in late 1777. Other pressing concerns occupied the public. These separate issues influenced each other, interacting, shaping opinion, and their coverage in newspapers and sermons heightened doubts about the progress of the war and the personal sacrifices it demanded. In our terms, Cambridge faced what might be called the revolutionary challenge of the Second Day. In this more sober environment, ordinary men and women revisited the demands of living in a society that had rejected British monarchy and all that went with it. Two years after Bunker Hill, what did it mean, they asked, to proclaim independence? What kind of society did independence yield? Daily annoyances on Prospect Hill were part of this complex conversation. In this context, Heath and Burgoyne spent a long winter arguing about national responsibility and honor. The complexity of their exchanges restores to the revolutionary story the dark moments between the Declaration of Independence and the end of the war when Americans—not just those living in Massachusetts—were uncertain where their political experiment would take them.

For one thing, the war had not gone well. The victory at Saratoga was welcome news, of course, but that event could hardly offset Washington's desperate situation in Pennsylvania. American forces had failed to stop General Howe from retaking Philadelphia. While his army occupied that city, Washington struggled to endure a hard winter at Valley Forge. We know that Burgoyne's surrender helped persuade the French in 1778 to recognize the independence of the United States, but the people who had to accommodate a huge prison camp in their community could not have forecast an alliance that did in fact change the course of the Revolution. A more immediate concern was the possibility that the British might organize a naval attack on Boston or, more likely, march north from their base in Newport, Rhode Island. In such an event, no one could be certain about controlling six thousand enemy soldiers.

The challenge of independence presented itself in another, more significant way. It was not that war-weary citizens of Massachusetts wanted to restore their status as colonists or subjects of George III. Rather, independence was an abstraction, something highly valued but requiring definition by the people who so enthusiastically proclaimed it. After all, a newly independent nation—as we have witnessed throughout the modern world—could adopt different forms of government and still take pride in liberating itself from imperial rule. By and large, Americans thought that independence involved the will of the people. In Massachusetts, during the long winter of 1777–78, the process of restructuring civil society centered on approving a constitution that reflected the state's revolutionary goals. In June 1777, the legislature "resolved itself into a convention to draw up a new form of government." After days of squabbling about details, the political leaders presented the result to the towns. If they expected swift approval, they were in for a rude surprise.[12]

The people overwhelmingly rejected the document. The reasons for such a negative reaction varied from town to town. Some demanded a convention—a special elected group completely separate from the sitting legislature—to draft a proper constitution. Others protested the lack of a bill of rights. The proposed organization of the state militia raised doubts. But at a moment when Americans—at least in the Northern states—were contemplating the character of a new revolutionary society, many towns in Massachusetts reaffirmed the principle that all men are created equal. They spurned the idea that potential citizens should be excluded from the franchise because of the color of their skin.

Several examples stand out. Sutton, a small village a few miles south of Worcester, used the occasion to condemn the entire commerce in enslaved people. How, they exclaimed in their return, could the state condone this trade "when the poor innocent Affricans who never hurt or offered any Injury or Insult to this country have been so unjustly assaulted inhumanely Murdered many of them"? Sutton also denounced a system that deprived "the original Natives of the Land [of] the Privileges of Man." The residents of Georgetown, a village north of Salem, expressed themselves even more passionately. They instructed the legislature that there was no justification for "a Man being born in Africa, India, or ancient America or even being much Sun burnt [to be] deprived of having a Vote for Representative." Cambridge turned down the proposed constitution by a vote of 79 to 0. While the town meeting did not mention racial discrimination, we know that residents were appalled when they learned—perhaps incorrectly—that British soldiers on Prospect Hill had murdered a Black boy.[13]

Burgoyne's arrival in Cambridge also coincided with a deeply disturbing controversy over the fundamental values of the new republic. The problem had nothing to do with loyalists who rejected the whole idea of independence. Local committees of safety and observation had removed any serious threat from disgruntled Tories. An entirely different peril had become apparent throughout the state sometime in mid-1777, and war-weary Americans blamed other Americans—neighbors, acquaintances, individuals they saw every day, who had once enthusiastically supported resistance to Great Britain but who, as the fighting continued, came to view the conflict as an opportunity to make a lot of money without much concern for the welfare of their fellow revolutionaries.

No doubt, wars encourage a few fellow travelers to conflate patriotism and greed. At such moments, self-seeking becomes betrayal, and the public shows no sympathy for arguments claiming that free markets are the best mechanism for establishing fair prices. American revolutionaries had no patience for such reasoning. They had made personal and economic sacrifices to secure independence, and now, the selfish behavior of a new class of speculators and profiteers made a mockery of the common cause.[14]

The internal enemies went by several names—monopolists, forestallers, and, most often, extortionists. Whatever the specific term, these practices involved placing the interests of the individual over those of the community. In 1777, one Massachusetts minister depicted extortion as a sin "whereby a person who has anything to sell, taking advantage of his neighbor's necessity, [and] requires more for it than a reasonable price." He defended a moral economy, a concept rooted in the religious culture of late medieval Europe. The ordinary farm families throughout the Cambridge region agreed, condemning the "locusts and canker worms, in human form, who have increased, proceeded along the road to plunder." In even more emphatic language, the Reverend William Gordon concluded, "If men in this day will not be content with a livelihood, and ill make themselves fortunes, immense fortunes, out of the distress of the people, I say, let the curse of heaven fall upon their substance, their unhallowed gains."[15]

We know that these apparent threats to the Revolution soon passed, giving way to new challenges. Washington kept his ragtag army together at Valley Forge, finding ways to fight another day. After many contentious town meetings, the people of Massachusetts eventually managed to ratify a constitution. A few years later, state courts outlawed slavery. And the fear of scheming extortionists dissipated over time. Transient concerns of this sort are not usually the focus of popular narratives of the American Revolution. During the winter of 1777, however, they were fundamental, the social context shaping how an anxious community confronted the British prisoners on Prospect Hill.

* * *

The Revolutionary War transformed the physical appearance of Prospect Hill. Almost as far back as the seventeenth century it was farmland. But when George Washington organized the siege of Boston in 1775, the Hill suddenly became the site of dozens of military barracks. One map from that period shows a somewhat schematic rendering of an American fortification. From this elevated position the Americans kept track of the movement of General Gage's troops in Boston.

Surveillance worked in the other direction as well. Archibald Robertson, a talented artist and a lieutenant in the Royal Engineers, spent free time during the British occupation of Boston drawing landscapes of the area. No doubt, he and his commanders simply wanted to know what the Americans were doing. One remarkable drawing completed in 1776—well before Burgoyne's arrival—reveals the location of Washington's hastily constructed barracks. It is doubtful that much changed over the next several months, except of course, that the temporary housing intended originally for the American troops had fallen into disrepair. An officer reported soon after the British abandoned Boston, "notwithstanding [the] Care [that] has bin Taken to Nail up the Barracks as the Soldiers are ordered out, I find many of them Brook open Whereby they are Exposed To Much Dammage from Winds & Weather. Also, many Poor familys on Winter & Prospect Hills Removed into sd Barracks."[16]

American officers oversaw the construction of many more barracks on Prospect Hill and Winter Hill. The quality did not improve.

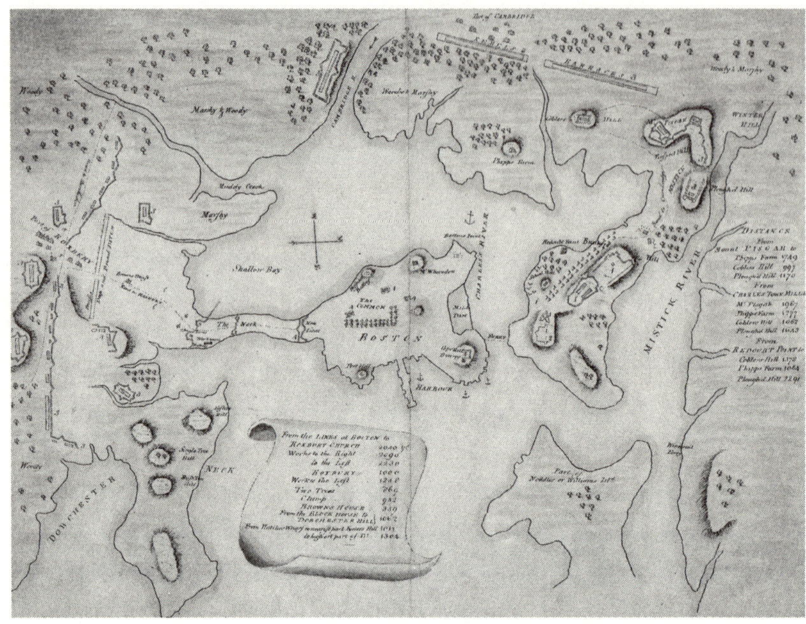

Map of Boston Harbor during the British occupation. The buildings on Prospect Hill are shown near the upper righthand corner. Manuscript map of the Battle of Bunker Hill, attr. S. Biggs, November 1775. (Collection of the Massachusetts Historical Society)

German soldiers were assigned to Winter Hill. That decision seems to have been made in deference to the British, who insisted on keeping Major General Riedesel's soldiers separate. The Germans accepted his situation, and during their imprisonment, they pragmatically tried to avoid disputes with Americans. Not so the British. As one German officer explained, "A great deal of animosity exists between the American and English soldiers, and a number of encounters that have taken place between them have made our stay here still more irksome and unbearable."[17]

Vexing encounters were only part of the problem. With so many people coming and going—providing food and other services, for example—it proved almost impossible to police the boundaries of the camps. Heath tried, ordering "no inhabitant of the United States, or any other person whatever, shall at any time enter the

Lieutenant Archibald Robertson's view of Prospect Hill from Boston in 1776. The American position is marked by a flag. (New York Public Library, Spencer Collection)

limits assigned for preventing their communication with the prisoners, without written license obtained for that purpose."[18] One rule invited no negotiation. The Americans absolutely prohibited prisoners from visiting Boston—always an enticing possibility for British troops with too much time on their hands.

Boston itself posed an additional problem. Continental officers such as Washington worried that one of Burgoyne's soldiers might mingle with local people and gather sensitive military intelligence, which they would share when they returned to England. In November 1777, Samuel Adams, then serving in the Continental Congress, expressed a hope that "Burgoyne will not be permitted to reside in Boston; for if he is, I fear that inconsiderate persons of fashion and some significance will be induced under the idea of Politeness to form connections with him, dangerous to the public."[19] Adams need not have worried. The people he had in mind were not Tories but, rather, Americans who did not comprehend the full meaning of cultural independence. Heath made certain that Burgoyne stayed in Cambridge.

The situation on Prospect Hill deteriorated rapidly. British soldiers desperate to keep warm cut down almost all the trees, leaving the camp during a wet season muddy and bare. With several thousand troops and dependents living there, other troublesome issues soon arose. No witness specifically mentioned sanitation, but the threat of disease—not to mention noxious smells—must have been on everyone's mind. The barracks were small, cramped, and poorly lit. Surviving from day to day was an ordeal. One person claimed, "The barracks are without foundations, and built on boards, through which the rain and snow penetrate from all sides."[20] A British sergeant echoed the complaint. "We reached the barracks on Prospect Hill very late in the evening," he wrote, "which were unfortunately in the worst condition imaginable from the inclemency of the weather." He and his men "were obliged to cut down the rafters of our room to dry ourselves."[21]

American guards inflamed a volatile situation. Heath insisted that securing the Convention Army required between 1,000 and 1,200 men. Since most regular Continental troops remained with Gates in New York after Saratoga or were serving with Washington near Philadelphia, the responsibility for overseeing the activities on Prospect Hill fell to local militia units and a handful of experienced American officers such as Colonel David Henley. Almost all militiamen were farmers—some were boys as young as fourteen—who had no special training as guards. The Germans described them as "working men."[22] Whatever their occupations may have been, they faced a formidable challenge. The ratio of prisoners to guards was approximately six to one. The major task for the Americans was maintaining "a chain of sentries" around the camp, a lonely, often boring duty as sentinels that left individual soldiers exposed during emergencies. For some the task was too much, and they took off for home. Washington advised Heath to recruit militiamen from towns in the western part of the state, since the distance from their farms would discourage absenteeism.[23]

British prisoners often ridiculed the Americans. One of Burgoyne's sergeants reported "continued broils with the American guards, which are composed of militia, who not being under very great discipline, not only infringe their orders, which they perhaps do not comprehend, or else use their authority as they think proper." He added that it was amusing to witness the guards during their rounds: "You will see an old man of sixty, and a boy of sixteen; a Black and an old decrepit man, limping by his side." These ridiculous characters seemed to have stepped out of a sketch by the renowned satirist William Hogarth or the play by Burgoyne. But as the sergeant admitted, it was dangerous to cross these rustics: "They are ready enough in presenting their pieces, and if a [British] soldier come the least near them they level at him, and say, 'I swear now, if you attempt to pass, I'll blaze at you.'"[24]

The pieces the Americans presented were firelocks, a generic term for long guns that required a spark from flint or steel to ignite the powder. Several different guns at the time qualified as firelocks. Even in the army there was no standard-issue weapon. Many militiamen brought their own guns, but as late as April 1778 an American officer guarding the camps petitioned the Massachusetts government for more firelocks, since eighteen of the American soldiers had no guns at all.[25]

Firelocks with smooth bores were awkward to handle. They measured between five and six feet and weighed about ten pounds. For a sentry on guard duty these were adequate weapons, and over the period that the Convention Army resided in Cambridge, several British soldiers who ignored commands from the Americans were shot. Nevertheless, when the militiamen were operating in close quarters—perhaps when they were crowded by unhappy prisoners—the firelocks were unwieldy and could be easily knocked away. What made all the difference for controlling the camps were sharp bayonets, which transformed the guns into spears. For Americans marching in close quarters—often near groups of British prisoners—bayonets proved a very effective instrument for maintaining order.

As one might expect, daily life in the camps was boring. Some Germans looking for money worked for local farmers. There is no record of the British doing so. Some prisoners simply ran away,

American soldiers (riflemen) in uniform, Daniel Chodowiecki, engraved by Daniel Berger, 1784. (From *Allgemeines historisches Taschenbuch, oder Abriss der merkwürdigsten neuen Welt-Begebenheiten: enthaltend für 1784 die Geschichte der Revolution von Nord-America,* by M. C. Sprengel; John Hay Library at Brown University, Anne S. K. Brown Military Collection)

hoping to rejoin British forces stationed in New York City. Others accepted offers to serve in the American army. Burgoyne chastised the Americans for allowing his troops to switch sides, a practice also denounced by Continental officers, but recruiters always found the possibility of filling the ranks with new men tempting.[26]

British soldiers could leave the confines of Prospect Hill if they obtained an official pass from an American officer. The regulation failed to keep prisoners from milling around Cambridge. James Haden, an English prisoner, reported, "The great number of Soldiers that have been permitted to flock to Town, have been productive of many irregularities, and gives the public a bad impression of the Discipline of the British Troops."[27] The regulars soon discovered how to counterfeit the required papers, and not a few confrontations occurred when suspicious American sentries challenged the authenticity of the passes. No doubt, the British were drawn to town in search of whisky, which, legal or not, they purchased at local taverns. The trade was hard to control. The Massachusetts House of Representatives responded to the problem by prohibiting the sale of "any Spirits, Distilled Wine, Ale, Beer or Cyder, to any of the British or Foreign troops within a mile of the Camps at Winter or Prospect Hill."[28] It was even said that the British soldiers tarrying in taverns corrupted Harvard students, but one suspects that in such matters the boys did not need encouragement. Heath wrote directly to Burgoyne about "a Billiard Table" that British officers set up "in a house near the center of the Town of Cambridge & that company is frequently there at very unseasonable hours." He added gratuitously that this entertainment disturbed the inhabitants.[29]

The order to remain in camp made little difference. British soldiers had no trouble smuggling whisky into the barracks, and drunkenness may have explained the destruction of several barracks as well as the incident that led to Henley's court-martial. British prisoners may have set fire to one of the barracks. Such threats put authorities throughout the area on high alert.[30] In January 1778, officials reported it was "highly probable" that many British prisoners "are now lurking in this Town [Boston] for no good purposes and that it is the duty of this Court to See that Proper care be taken to find out evil disposed persons and prevent them from having it in their power to injure us." The court instructed Heath to conduct a thorough sweep of the city to discover "where such Evil-minded Persons may likely be harboured." One hopes that he was able to find Thomas Silk, alias Old Ginger, a British sailor about forty years old, "a deceitful villain, often shewing his private parts."[31]

Although British soldiers lurking around Cambridge may have been tiresome—there were no reports of assaults on Americans—they had a huge negative impact on the local economy. The most pressing problem was firewood. Householders competed with the prisoners for limited fuel. Heath felt obliged to provide sufficient wood for Burgoyne's army, and he did his best to find reliable sources from as far away as New Hampshire. The supply never fulfilled demand. Heath warned Washington that any delay in sending the British back to England "will greatly distress the Inhabitants both as to provisions and Fuel, especially the latter, [since] Wood is now twelve & fourteen Dollars per Cord on the wharves, and the Inhabitants cannot obtain a supply at that price."[32]

But they tried. Ordinary people found ways to short-circuit the system. The Massachusetts General Assembly urged the selectmen of Boston to assist Heath in providing wood for the British. "Every vessel coming in from the eastward [now Maine] for this purpose," the legislature ordered, "[must] be furnished with a pass signed by General Heath, certifying that the wood in those vessels is for the sole use of the army with General Burgoyne." It added that if the wood is "taken the army must be the sufferers."[33] Americans attempting to keep their families warm during an extremely cold winter probably did not have a lot of sympathy for the suffering prisoners. The competition for wood triggered serious inflation. Hannah Winthrop estimated that the Convention Army required "Two hundred and fifty cords of wood" every week. "Think then," she observed, "how we must be distressed. Wood has risen to €5 10s [5 pounds, ten shillings] per cord, and but a little to be purchased."[34]

As the weeks passed, people in Cambridge expressed a range of emotions—desperation, fear, and depression. If the British had followed the German example and paid greater attention to the sensitivities of the Americans, a volatile situation might have yielded little more than grumbling. But they could not help themselves. Even as prisoners they viewed the king's former subjects as lesser beings. And because of behavior often perceived as arrogance, they inspired comparisons. If these visitors were the products of an aristocratic society, they invited Americans to reflect on their own culture—on the meaning of independence. In her letters to Mercy Otis Warren, Winthrop voiced anger and despair. She informed her friend that "the British officers live in the most luxurious manner possible, rioting on the fat of the land, and talking at large with the self-importance of lords of the soil." Everywhere she encountered arrogance, soldiers "Prancing & Patrolling every corner of the town, ornamented with their glittering side arms, weapons of destruction." Words failed to capture "our unhappy circumstances." What could one do in these circumstances? "Who is to plead our cause?" she asked. The prospect was dispiriting: "For my part I think, insults, famine & a train of evils present [themselves] to view."[35]

Another, even more contentious issue inflamed public opinion. Everyone knew how horribly the British in New York City dealt with captured American soldiers. Newspapers regularly reported the atrocities. The enemy condemned thousands of prisoners to needless suffering on rotting vessels anchored in the harbor. Large numbers died on these floating coffins. The comparison with how Heath cared for the welfare of Burgoyne's army was striking, certainly insulting to the people who witnessed events on Prospect Hill. One newspaper noted that Americans—even "the lower class of people"—had tried to treat the British prisoners with "humanity."[36]

Care of the prisoners became a measure of America's sense of honor. Ministers assured their congregations that they should be proud not to have taken Britain as the model for proper behavior. On November 18, 1777—soon after Burgoyne arrived in Cambridge—the Reverend Israel Evans schooled his parishioners in Concord about the comparison between the two cultures. "Cowards insult those who fall into their hands," he said, "but the brave are compassionate, and fight no longer than there is absolute necessity." An honorable nation does not humiliate its enemies, especially when they are most vulnerable. The proof could be seen on Prospect Hill. "Let General Burgoyne, and his officers generously speak the truth," Evans continued, "and bear witness that nothing was wanting, on the part of the noble spirited General Gates, and his officers, to render them as happy as possible, and even make them forget they were conquered." No one could doubt that "we treated them much more mildly, than we should be treated in a similar situation."[37]

Such honorable behavior strained the capacity for goodwill at Cambridge. How could one ignore "the insolence peculiar to British troops, who conceive themselves to be the chosen of the world, and the idea of superiority over Americans, having long been used to consider them and speak of them as their subjects?"[38] A writer identified as "Candidus" reminded journal readers that they had been forced to watch as "Beef, Pork Wood, etc. have been for several days carting to the barracks in Cambridge, for the subsistence of General Burgoyne's army." Revolutionaries in Massachusetts must surely pity "our poor countrymen, who have fallen into the hands of the inhuman General Howe." These troops who fought for independence were "carried through the city of New York, and treated with all the insult possible; were afterwards thrown into large store houses, where they remained for days without any subsistence, and kept there 'till near two thirds of 'em perish'd—Blush Britons! Blush!"[39]

* * *

General Burgoyne would surely have disagreed with the Reverend Evans. He most assuredly could not overlook the fact that his army had been defeated. He was reminded every day that he was a prisoner. As the weeks passed in Cambridge, Burgoyne's list of humiliations—real or imagined—grew. It seemed to him as if the Americans were determined to renegotiate, or simply to ignore, the articles of surrender that stipulated how the Convention Army should be treated on its journey back to England. It was hard to separate these complaints from personal concerns. Burgoyne had not anticipated being trapped in Massachusetts. Delay meant that he could not defend himself against enemies in London who brayed for a full investigation of his failure at Saratoga. The stress of imprisonment took a toll on his health.

As hope of quickly returning to England faded, annoyance fueled anger. Burgoyne complained to Heath, appealed to Washington, sent protests to Gates, and asked Congress to intervene. Almost all of Burgoyne's discontent reflected conflicting interpretations of the original surrender agreement signed at Saratoga. The various grievances generated separate, although complementary negotiations, and often before the parties had dealt with one problem, another came to the fore. The difficulty of sending and receiving messages during wartime added to the confusion in Cambridge. Washington was hundreds of miles away from Prospect Hill, and while Heath remained in Boston, he often had to confer with Washington or Congress before making decisions. These exchanges often took weeks, and by the time someone resolved a contentious issue, Burgoyne had raised a different one. More significant for our story, ordinary Americans followed these squabbles—perhaps without knowing the full details at any moment—forming their own ideas about the merits of British complaints.

The first controversy centered on the place and timing of departure. Burgoyne insisted that the entire Convention Army should sail from Boston. As soon as possible. And, of course, that had been the understanding at Saratoga. Washington, however, remained deeply skeptical of the plan. He believed that the whole idea was a clever scheme allowing the British to dispatch new troops to America for every one who returned to England. Although Congress exercised authority over Burgoyne's forces, Washington urged the departure be delayed as long as possible. Since the British could not be trusted, he explained to Heath, "policy & a regard to our own interest are strongly opposed to our adopting or pursuing any measure to facilitate their [the Convention troops'] embarkation & passage Home."[40] His opinions were not easily ignored. Weather worked in his favor, for during the harsh months of winter, it seemed unlikely that a large number of British transports would be able to reach Boston. Moreover, welcoming so many enemy ships into the harbor raised issues of military security.

Washington also predicted that once Burgoyne recognized the difficulty of a swift Boston departure, he would turn his attention to Newport, Rhode Island, a city then occupied by the British. He was correct. Burgoyne insisted that a shift from one port to another did not violate the Convention articles. On this point, he argued for a flexible interpretation of the treaty with Gates. The alteration in plan involved only a minor detail. Not so, retorted Washington. He reminded Heath that if Burgoyne was allowed to sail from Newport, he might decide that the destination was not England but rather New York City, where Howe, commander of the British forces in America, would welcome several thousand new troops. We now know that Washington's skepticism was entirely justified. Howe did, in fact, put forward a devious plan to divert the Convention Army to New York. Although people in Cambridge may have been suspicious of Burgoyne's request, they did not know of Howe's proposition. His scheme remained secret for more than a century.[41] Even without damning evidence, Washington advised Heath and others that it was unwise to trust the British.

Washington feared that the situation in Cambridge might turn violent. He predicted that several thousand enemy troops—their hopes of returning suddenly dashed—could be tempted to organize a massive breakout, putting the American guards in danger. Washington advised Heath, "I would therefore have you increase the vigilance and if necessary, the strength of your Guards. All Magazines of arms should be removed from Boston and its neighbourhood, for if any attempt is made, it must be by first seizing upon arms to force their way."[42] However justified Washington's alarm may have been, the prisoners did not attempt a large-scale escape. The threat, however, seemed real enough, and the residents of Cambridge became increasingly anxious about so many unhappy enemy soldiers remaining on Prospect Hill.

Querulous exchanges between Heath and Burgoyne occurred almost daily. Burgoyne protested when the Americans demanded a complete listing of all his troops. Since they were technically on parole, the request made sense to Congress. Without detailed information about each soldier before departure, he could easily return to fight again. Collection posed an impossible challenge. Congress expected Heath "to cause to be taken down the name and rank of every commissioned officer, and the name, former place of abode and occupation, size, age, and description of every non-commissioned officer and private soldier."[43]

Burgoyne refused to cooperate, insisting the order had no precedent in military protocol. In addition, the entire episode cast doubt on British honor by suggesting his troops might cheat their parole agreement. Suggestions of this sort, he insisted, amounted to an insult upon his country.[44] Whether the British would have cheated is hard to judge. One wonders how the plan could have been implemented. Even in modern times, aided by computer searches, it would be extremely difficult to link specific British soldiers on Prospect Hill with small towns in England and Scotland. When Heath begged for relief, Congress offered no help. It praised his efforts—however ineffective—while also noting that the goal in "this important business . . . [is preserving] on one side, the faith and honour of these infant States . . . and on the other, the magnanimity and resolution of Congress."[45] The American reluctance to push the issue is revealing. It exposed surprising sensitivity to the charge that the newly independent nation might not in fact be acting in an honorable manner. The dispute over the census was never resolved—a pity since such a list would have contained valuable data about the health, appearance, and mobility of ordinary eighteenth-century people.

The squabbling about the details of the Convention agreement might have resulted in little more than hard feelings. That did not happen. Suddenly, ongoing grumbling between Burgoyne and the American authorities sparked a crisis that eventually involved the entire nation. The controversy did not originally seem to be more than an annoyance. From the moment Burgoyne arrived in Cambridge, he complained that the housing provided by Heath for the British officers was inadequate—indeed, insulting for soldiers of senior rank.[46] He had a point, at least during the early days. He reported, "After being pressed into Cambridge through bad weather, inconvenience and fatigue, without any preparation made to receive the superior officers, I was lodged in a miserable public-house [a local tavern]."[47] The charge embarrassed Heath. It was not that he worried about Burgoyne's physical comfort. Rather, as the Continental officer in charge, he knew housing the British was his responsibility.

Heath encountered obstructions at every turn. There were simply not enough houses in the area to meet the unexpected demand. Heath did not have legal authority to evict householders—something he would have been reluctant to do in any case—and neither the state government nor the representatives of Harvard College showed much interest in solving the problem. Heath begged for cooperation. "The honor of the State is in danger," he reminded the governing council of Massachusetts, "the public Faith responsible—circumstances will no longer admit of delay—decisive measures must be immediately adopted."[48] The response was more foot-dragging. To complicate the situation, potential landlords often demanded exorbitant rents. Since Burgoyne insisted that he was not a prisoner of war—only the leader of a paroled army passing through Cambridge on its way to England—he was obliged to pay for lodging out of British funds. Locals knew that they would be compensated by the British in hard currency, something in short supply in a country relying on badly inflated paper money.

Heath's efforts failed to placate Burgoyne. The British general did not do much better on his own. He attempted to negotiate lodging with local landlords, but the houses on offer were ill-furnished and in poor repair. "The only prospect that remains to me personally," he groused, "is that I shall be permitted to occupy a House without a Table, Chair or any other Article of Furniture for the Price of an hundred and Fifty pounds sterling." The rent seemed outrageous. He told Heath that such an exorbitant sum "would have been required for a palace in the dearest metropolis of the world."[49]

Burgoyne refused to compromise. In a letter to Heath dated November 10, 1777, he insisted the lodging available in Cambridge was "unfit for gentlemen in their situation in any part of the world."[50] Again, there was a suggestion that the king's former subjects in America were not quite civilized. Although Heath did not have much experience engaging palaces in distant places, he responded: In reference "to the quarters allotted to the officers being such as would not be held fit for gentlemen in their situation in any part of the world . . . your Excellency may have seen jails preferable, yet I can assure you that the same quarters were built for, allotted to, and occupied by, our officers of the same rank for their winter quarters, and they were easy and contented in them."[51]

Within a month Heath had sorted out the problem. Burgoyne rented an impressive house formerly owned by a loyalist who had fled when the British abandoned Boston. Indeed, during the American siege of Boston after Bunker Hill, it had been the official residence of General Israel Putnam, a leading officer in the Continental Army. General Riedesel and his wife were quite pleased with their cottage and immediately planted a garden. Even so, Riedesel told Burgoyne, "We cannot deny that we are astonished at observing the care that has been taken of the lodgings of the English general officers, while we have not even been thought of."[52] Cambridge residents shared the German general's irritation. Not surprisingly, ordinary people in Massachusetts began to ask, "If they [the British] are thus insolent now they are prisoners, what would they be were they our masters?"[53] It was a fair question. The day-to-day experience of living with the enemy reminded Americans—at least, in Cambridge—what it meant no longer to be British.

• CHAPTER 5 •

Breach of Public Faith

The autumn of 1777 marked the season of America's discontent. The Continental Congress was on the run—literally.[1] After the British General William Howe occupied Philadelphia, the legislators—some of the country's most prominent revolutionary leaders—fled for safety. The vulnerability of Congress was embarrassing, but the prospect of having the British take American congressmen prisoner was unthinkable. The legislators fled first to Lancaster, Pennsylvania, about one hundred miles west of Philadelphia. That location soon proved insecure, and the representatives crossed the Susquehanna River, where they met in a modest building in York—the revolutionary capital of the United States of America.[2]

The risk of capture was only part of the problem. From the beginning of the war, Congress struggled raising funds to support the army. Inflation was out of control. The representatives of the separate states found it hard to cooperate. In the midst of these major challenges, Congress attempted to draft a constitution for the United States. The document it produced after a long debate was adopted in November 1777. The result was dispatched to all thirteen states including Massachusetts. Because of deep political divisions, however, the states did not ratify the Articles of Confederation until 1781.

Despite these seemingly intractable problems, Congress forged ahead. It had no other choice. At this low point in the Revolution, it embodied the fragile hope for the survival of the republican experiment. If by some misfortune the British had managed to destroy an institution that served as a beacon of American resistance to imperial rule, the Revolution might have come to a very swift and dispiriting end. George Washington was in no position to protect Congress. The Continental Army could hardly feed and clothe American troops at Valley Forge. Although critics ridiculed the weakness of Congress, it deserved praise for governing at all. Communication with scattered military commanders and distant state officials took weeks, sometimes a month, and the flow of information was vulnerable to interruption by the enemy.

Even more impressive at this critical moment was the ability of General John Burgoyne, an American prisoner of war, after all, to dominate legislative business. By sheer force of personality, he commanded attention. Although he was in Cambridge, nearly four hundred miles from York, he repeatedly created problems the overworked congressmen could not ignore. The hastily negotiated agreement General Gates had signed at Saratoga was the source of the problem. The loosely drawn articles of surrender invited interpretation. Burgoyne treated it as a formal treaty. No detail could be changed. Although the Americans took a more pragmatic view of the various articles of the Convention, they recognized that the document raised sensitive military and diplomatic topics.

Still, Burgoyne's grousing strained patience. Reports from Cambridge informed the members of Congress that the British general refused to provide detailed data about the prisoners, whined about the condition of housing, and made threatening pronouncements about his plans for leaving Massachusetts on a fleet of British transports. All this mattered. But the underlying challenge for Congress was largely strategic. Would six thousand British troops somehow be reunited with Howe's forces? The question provoked touchy questions about national honor, a pressing concern at the moment.

Congress's almost obsessive fear that it might betray honor energized the entire debate at York. The concept that focused their attention was not the concept of honor that Burgoyne and other military figures associated with personal reputation—as when they insisted that they were honorable men. Rather, congressional delegates understood that international credit relations depended on honor. At the time, most commercial transactions were negotiated through bills of credit, personal pledges to pay an obligation by a stated date. In the absence of a reliable banking system, merchants could not have survived without these mutual promises. As Charles Davenant, an Englishman who pioneered a new field known as "political arithmetic," observed, "Of all beings that have existence only in the minds of men, nothing is more fantastical and nice than Credit; it is never to be forced; it hangs upon *opinion;* it depends upon our passions of hope and fear; it comes many times unsought for, and often goes away without reason; and when once lost, is hardly to be quite recovered."[3]

The entire financial network depended on mutual trust. It is not surprising that eighteenth-century religious groups such as the Quakers sought out fellow church members in distant ports on the assumption that coreligionists could be trusted in business more than could strangers. As soon as the United States declared independence, Congress realized it desperately needed large loans from European countries such as Holland to support the war effort. Since the new republic had almost no collateral to support these agreements—states contributed some funds, but these were seldom sufficient for the purpose—Congress pledged its honor to cover long-term debts. Burgoyne's surprising and unwelcome actions in Cambridge threatened these delicate arrangements. Although congressional representatives saw the British general as little more than a passing annoyance, they moved quickly to secure the nation's honor.

A remarkable letter written during the Burgoyne debate reveals the tensions between a commitment to national honor and the demands of realpolitik. From York, Eliphalet Dyer, a representative from Connecticut, informed the state's governor, Jonathan Trumbull Sr., about the details of the Burgoyne controversy. It was a good thing that Dyer was "very talkative," as John Adams privately claimed. From time to time, he may have bored Adams on the floor of Congress, but Adams concluded that Dyer "means well and judges well."[4] Dyer knew that the success of the Revolution was at stake, but even though so many problems confronted Congress, he concluded that "the most important & perplexing of all is the measures & conduct we ought to take with respect to Gennll. Burgoyne and his Army."

According to Dyer, the legislators recognized that they could resolve the dispute in Cambridge in two different ways. But unfortunately, the possible solutions were not only mutually exclusive but also raised serious risks to national reputation and security. As Dyer explained, "On the one hand there is everything to fear if he [Burgoyne] is suffered to embark that he will join the Enemy in America instead of going to Great Britain, on the other hand it concerns our inviolability to keep our faith, & maintain our honor, pledged for the punctual fulfillment on our part of all treaties."

Dyer understood the law of contracts. The logic was indisputable. A deal was a deal even if one of the parties later had second thoughts. Moreover, God enjoined honest behavior. And in addition to the Lord, others groups allegedly waited for the outcome. Dyer imagined a huge audience of Europeans skeptical of American independence and eagerly anticipating the new republic's failure to fulfill its own noble principles. The future had to be considered, since, as Dyer predicted, history would judge how Congress handled the Convention Army. As the Connecticut delegate explained to Governor Trumbull in convoluted syntax: "We would not offend Heaven by our perfidy, nor forfeit our honor & reputation in the eyes of this, or the European world, who are & will be most attentively watchful, over every part of our publick Conduct, and will fix their opinion & form their Estimation of these American States on no more than that which concerns our publick faith, & honor." The obligation to uphold moral principles in international affairs struck

Dyer as especially urgent, since the United States was only an "infant empire," and early policy mistakes would surely tarnish "a fair & reputable Carracter, which once lost is hardly to be regained."

Like the other congressmen, Dyer worried that pushing moral considerations about trust and honor might do real damage to America's interests. No one could deny that Burgoyne threatened the nation's military security. Of course, anticipating world opinion, Dyer also hoped no one would view America as a "perfidious rising Empire" if it kept Burgoyne's army from sailing to England. Pressure on Congress increased throughout the fall of 1777. News from Massachusetts suggested that Burgoyne intended to nullify the Convention agreement, and if he did so, he might attempt to join his troops with those already occupying New York. Such circumstances demanded a response. Should the Americans keep up their side of the Saratoga bargain? Was a battlefield settlement really a proper treaty or a legal contract? If not, what then was the justification for canceling Burgoyne's embarkation for Great Britain? Dyer assured Trumbull that "all the great writers on the law of Nature will vindicate us in a Suspension on our part." Learned treatises aside, doubts lingered. Dyer brooded over the possibility that Congress could not overcome its own biases in dealing with Burgoyne. After all, "in making up our Judgement, we are deeply interested, how to judge in our own Cause, our jealousies & Suspicions may goe too far, & warp our Judgements."[5]

The burden of making the honorable decision fell heavily on Henry Laurens. From November 1, 1777, to December 9, 1778, he served as the president of the Continental Congress. By all accounts he was a thoughtful, prudent man, much respected by Washington, and he served the Revolution at great personal sacrifice. Laurens was later taken prisoner by the British. After being released, he joined a distinguished team negotiating the treaty ending the Revolution. But however able Laurens was in political matters, his record as the owner of a large number of enslaved workers in South Carolina makes many modern Americans uncomfortable. Before the war he pioneered a coercive labor system that promised to increase the income of the state's rice planters. He devoted some of his scattered plantations solely to the production of food for the enslaved people on other Laurens holdings that focused entirely on growing rice for export. During the meetings of Congress at York, no one seems to have openly objected to how he had made a fortune.[6]

Soon after the Convention Army arrived in Cambridge, it fell to Heath to keep Laurens informed about the situation at the prison camp. It is significant that at no time during the Burgoyne crisis did Heath question the orders he received from Congress. Like Washington, he believed that, in a free republic, civil authority always took precedence over the interests and opinions of the country's military leaders. There could be no compromise. Although Heath never compared the American system to Great Britain's, he was well aware that on all matters of policy he reported to an elected congress and not a monarch such as George III. Laurens advised Heath to watch Burgoyne carefully. The American general should push Burgoyne to complete the census of enemy prisoners. At the same time, Laurens urged Heath not to insist too aggressively that the British pay their debts for food and supplies as prisoners. Although no one knew what was on Burgoyne's mind—always his advantage in dealing with the Americans—Laurens feared that an angry, frustrated Burgoyne might strike out on his own.[7]

The days passed with no clear determination. Burgoyne dragged his feet on almost every point. Congress knew that somehow it must stop the British army from returning to England, but they did not see how to halt the embarkation. As Laurens told Heath, the Americans were just buying time. Congress, Laurens explained, wanted to find an answer "without subjecting the honour of the House or of its Constituents to any unfavorable imputation from the World." For now, Heath had to rely on his own discretion, since in this unwelcome business "the faith & honour to these Infant States" was on one side, and "on the other the magnanimity & Resolution of Congress to be exemplified in guarding against frauds & deceptions of an enemy who has hitherto practiced without remorse every Act of violence, injustice & Cruelty in the prosecution of the present War."[8] In the meantime, John Rutledge gave Heath the proverbial pat on the back: Keep up the good work in Cambridge. He assured Heath that "Congress repose the utmost confidence in your address and abilities for conducting with propriety this important business."

* * *

Then, as if by miracle, Congress obtained a letter that dramatically altered the course of events. In mid-November, Burgoyne had a fit of pique. The kind of housing he had expected in Cambridge—the proper lodging for British officers he thought General Gates had promised at Saratoga—was not on offer. Moreover, in his opinion, the local Americans were not doing enough to solve the problem. It was in this emotional state that Burgoyne wrote directly to Gates on November 14, 1777, complaining of the humiliation he faced as a prisoner (he preferred being called a parolee or visitor just passing through Massachusetts). Gates forwarded the letter to York, where it was first read by Congress on December 18. Referring specifically to representatives of the Massachusetts government, Burgoyne wrote: "They do what they can; but while the Supreme Powers of the State are unable or unwilling to enforce their [orders], and the inhabitants want the hospitality to assist us without it, *the public faith is broke,* and we are the immediate sufferers."[9] The insolence of the Americans seemed to absolve him of any obligation to observe the agreement carefully negotiated at Saratoga. Burgoyne soon had second thoughts about his impulsive claim, insisting that his words should not have been taken literally. After all, during a moment of passion the complaint was just an ill-considered expression. It was too late. Congress seized on the letter, raising immediately the possibility that if Burgoyne had in fact voluntarily broken the Convention agreement, then perhaps the United States was justified in doing so as well. He solved the honor problem.

Congress charged a select committee to review all the evidence it possessed relative to the surrender and subsequent imprisonment of the Convention Army. This material included the entire official correspondence between Heath and Burgoyne. How the committee conducted the investigation is significant. It examined not only Burgoyne's complaints but also the degree to which American officials bore responsibility for the British general's grievances. Like experienced lawyers—which of course many members of the Congress were—they reviewed the merits of each allegation. They insisted that they would make recommendations only after "mature attention."[10]

Some issues, committee members discovered, could be passed over quickly. They accepted that Burgoyne's troops had probably not turned over all the military supplies stipulated by the Gates agreement. There were reports, for example, that cartouche boxes and "several articles of military accoutrements" had gone missing at the moment of surrender at Saratoga. Each British soldier carried a cartouche box in which he stored cartridges for a smoothbore musket. The loss or destruction of these articles was a relatively minor matter, but the inquiry allowed the committee to raise questions at the start about Burgoyne's character that echoed throughout the investigation. On this article, it concluded that "the Convention has not been strictly complied with on the part of General Burgoyne, agreeably to its true spirit and intention of the contracting parties." After all, the representatives asked rhetorically, how could one trust Burgoyne when the Americans had documented "so many instances of former fraud in the conduct of our enemies?"[11]

The second contentious issue involved the American demand that Burgoyne submit a detailed description of all soldiers who had surrendered at Saratoga. Washington and others argued that unless Congress received this information before the Convention Army departed for England, the enemy troops could easily slip back to the United States and strengthen General Howe's forces. Over several months—from November 1777 to January 1778—Heath demanded an accurate listing, and repeatedly, Burgoyne refused to cooperate.

He insisted that his agreement with Gates had not required sharing this data: "the name, former place of abode, occupation, size, age, and description of every non-commissioned officer and private soldier, and all other persons comprehended in the Convention of Saratoga."[12]

Burgoyne offered two excuses for his obstruction. First, by asking for this information, the Americans signaled a lack of trust in the British. Why, he wondered, was the possibility of cheating even under discussion? An honorable person such as Burgoyne would never condone deception. Second, he insisted that Congress was trying to add new conditions to the surrender that had not been discussed at Saratoga. In other words, after all parties agreed to the contract, the Americans wanted unilaterally to amend it. Congress dismissed both arguments. A census of the prisoners at Cambridge "cannot be considered as imposing any new condition, but as a measure naturally resulting from the articles of the convention, which the conquering party has a right to avail itself of, and which is strictly justifiable." It then added a stinging rebuke to Burgoyne, noting that the Americans might have trusted Burgoyne "had no just suspicion of the want of good faith in the party surrendering presented itself."[13]

Then there was the matter of housing in Cambridge for the British officers. Especially during the first weeks of imprisonment, Burgoyne bitterly complained that his living arrangements were substandard—certainly, much inferior for a person of his stature. The charge generated little sympathy in Congress. The committee observed that considering the destruction caused by war—the British had only recently evacuated Boston—it seemed unrealistic to expect the Americans to provide better lodging. What did Burgoyne expect after "the sudden and unexpected arrival of so large a body of troops, the concourse of strangers in and near Boston, the devastation and destruction occasioned by the British army, not long since blocked up in that town"? Local authorities had performed as well as they could under the circumstances. Barracks were in short supply. To be sure, the committee concluded, "the accommodation of General Burgoyne and his officers might not be such as the public could wish or expect," but these were not normal times.[14]

Point by point, the committee established to its own satisfaction that the Americans had attempted to fulfill the Saratoga bargain. The exigencies of war explained why they occasionally came up short. But nothing that had occurred in Cambridge justified Burgoyne's "charge of a breach of the public faith." The claim insulted the United States and could not be allowed to pass without a firm response. According to the select committee, "This charge of a breach of public faith is of a most serious nature, pregnant with alarming consequence, and deserves greater attention, as it is not dropped in a hasty expression, dictated by a sudden passion, but is delivered as a deliberate act of judgement." Burgoyne had triggered a confrontation, and now "the security which these States have had in his personal honor is hereby destroyed."[15]

The full Congress immediately took up the committee report, Laurens sitting in the chair, and after a short debate, on January 3, 1778, it devised a brilliant solution to the Burgoyne crisis, at once practical and self-protecting. The revolutionaries turned the entire affair over to the king of England. The decision stipulated that Burgoyne's army would not be allowed to leave the United States until the representatives of the United States obtained "a distinct and explicit ratification of the convention of Saratoga . . . [from] the court of Great Britain."[16] Of course, they knew the exchange would never happen. If George III accepted the proposal, he would have had to recognize the independence of the new republic, something he could not bring himself to do for another six years. The result pleased Laurens, who wrote to his son John, praising "the rectitude of the Act" and announcing, "I would rather lose my whole Estate, than hear a majority of dissenting Voices. The grand Resolve passed Nemine Con [no one contradicting]."[17]

Laurens owed his legislative success largely to his distinguished colleague John Witherspoon, who delivered a powerful speech before Congress explaining the moral responsibilities of the new country and the treacherous character of the British. Witherspoon was the only member of the Continental Congress who was an ordained minister. Born in Scotland, he established himself there as a leader of the evangelical wing of the Presbyterian Church. Although his theological views clashed with more moderate churchmen, he earned respect as a serious philosopher. In 1768 he accepted the presidency of a New Jersey college later known as Princeton. About his sympathies for a republican form of government, there was no doubt. Witherspoon signed the Declaration of Independence. He welcomed a new regime liberated from aristocratic privilege. At the time of his election, he stated, "The Congress is, properly speaking, the representative of the great body of the people of North America."[18]

At the start of his speech, Witherspoon reminded colleagues why the dispute with Burgoyne was so important for the reputation of the United States, even as it struggled to survive on the battlefield. Independence involved more than a political declaration. It assumed a moral burden. He appealed to history. It was the country's responsibility "to preserve its faith and honor in solemn contracts: and it is especially so to us, as representing the United States of America, associated so lately, and just beginning to appear on a public stage." The obligation was heavy, and as if he were prescient about future challenges to the nation's honor, Witherspoon stated, "As the interest of this continent is committed to our care, it is our duty, and it will be expected of us, that we give the utmost attention that the public suffer no injury by deception, or abuse and insult, on the part of our enemies."[19]

The fundamental question before Congress, therefore, was whether, in face of the evidence collected by the select committee, the United States was justified in refusing to allow the Convention Army to leave the country. Witherspoon confessed that some of the allegations against Burgoyne—hiding the cartouche boxes, for example—were "trifling and unessential." But that was beside the point. In his estimation the case before Congress did not turn on such details. The larger ethical issue was whether his countrymen could deal with Burgoyne without giving into their own biases about the general. Fair judgment required a recognition that "jealousy and suspicion" could prejudice their decision and expose their actions to accusations "of evasive and artful conduct."[20] Moreover, the historical record was clear. Sometimes victors mislead defeated enemies with false promises. It had happened in ancient Rome and in Scotland after the British crushed the Jacobite rising in 1745. This was precisely the kind of treachery that an honorable country must avoid.

How, then, should the United States proceed? What criterion should Congress employ in deciding whether it had acted fairly in the Burgoyne affair? How could it overcome biases fueled by resentment to yield fair judgment? It was at this point in his presentation that Witherspoon made a surprising move. He recognized that the Americans could develop a jurisprudential argument on the basis of learned treatises on "the law of nature and nations." They could "heap up citations from numerous writers on that subject."[21]

There was no need to do so. The fundamental issue before the representatives was the substance of "the law of nature," which in turn was "nothing else but the law of general reason, or those obligations of duty from reason to conscience, on one individual to another, antecedent to any particular law derived from the social compact, or even actual consent." For anyone at the time engaged in commerce, the observation sounded like common sense. Business agreements depended on reputation, on the honor of all parties to a contract. Without honor there could be no meaningful trust. For Witherspoon, international law—the relation of one nation to another—was nothing more than an extension of how individuals judged one another in everyday affairs. As he explained, "One nation to another is just as man to man in a state of nature." Settlement of complex disputes on any level required the application of everyday experience: "Keeping this in view, a person of integrity will pass as sound a judgment on subjects of this kind, by consulting his own heart, as by turning over books and systems. The chief use of books and systems is, to apply the principle to particular cases and suppositions differently classed, and to point out the practice of nations in several minute and special particulars, which unless ascertained by practice, would be very uncertain and ambiguous."[22]

Within this framework—justice based on the dictates of the heart—it followed that ordinary Americans could see that the case against Burgoyne involved a lot more than evidence of fraud. Whether the specific accusations against him were true or not mattered not at all. People could argue endlessly about how to interpret details. Was the housing offered in Cambridge appropriate for someone "accustomed to the splendor of the British court, and possessed with ideas of his own importance" or not? The larger issue—really the universal element—was how the contending parties viewed the nature of contracts. Burgoyne insisted that because the Americans had failed to fulfill the Saratoga agreement, "the public faith is broken." He felt wronged. But, as Witherspoon told Congress, "The simplest man in the world knows, that a mutual onerous contract is always conditional; and that if the condition fails one side, whether from necessity or fraud, the other is free." That logic meant congressmen could and should assume that Burgoyne now believed himself liberated from further obligation to the Americans. He was free to pursue his own agenda. Indeed, as Witherspoon noted, Burgoyne would be a "fool" if he did not.[23]

The undeniable conclusion from Witherspoon's argument was that if Burgoyne no longer saw himself as bound by the articles of a contract, he became a danger to the security of the country. With no enforceable agreement in place, future dealings with Burgoyne depended not on law but on character. A focus on an assessment of moral qualities raised new questions. Was the man who claimed a "breach of faith" on frivolous grounds to be trusted? Witherspoon admitted that he had never met Burgoyne—although he did mention that he had visited England himself—but on the basis of "reading his lofty and sonorous proclamation, and some other productions," he assured Congress that Burgoyne "is evidently a man showy, vain, impetuous, and rash." One might wonder how this minister in the political forum squared a demand for an unbiased judgment in the Burgoyne affair with an obvious contempt for the man. Witherspoon insisted Burgoyne's flawed character compelled the American legislature to ask, "Do you think that such a man would not take the advantage of this pretended breach of the convention on our part; and endeavour to wipe off the reproach of his late ignominious surrender by some signal or desperate undertaking?"[24] Well, of course not. Accepting Witherspoon's tortured argument, verging on sophistry, Congress voted to prohibit Burgoyne's departure.

Although he was pleased with the results at York, President Laurens still worried about appearances. How would people far removed from the nation's temporary capital interpret the Burgoyne decision? Would they fail to see that Congress had taken the high moral ground rather than engaging in the kinds of casuistry associated with nations that did not define the burden of independence as the Americans did? During January 1778, Laurens dispatched letters to all thirteen state governments explaining the repudiation of the Saratoga agreement. The tone was defensive, as if something had gone wrong. For example, he informed George Clinton, governor of New York, about "a very solemn & important Act of Congress of the 8th Inst. For suspending the embarkation of Lieut. General Burgoyne & his Troops." The final decision came only "after long & dispassionate considerations judged to be equally justifiable & necessary." That being the case, Laurens expressed confidence that the resolution "will be confirmed by the approbation of all their Constituents in these United States who are most concerned, that the Justice & good Policy of the Act will be acknowledged by every disinterested Court in Europe."[25] Laurens may have been worried about soliciting loans from countries such as the Netherlands, but it is significant that he imagined large numbers of Americans, who were not in the room, worrying about how Europeans interpreted the Burgoyne affair.

The president appealed to revolutionary military leaders, asking if they had reservations about the treatment of Burgoyne. He assumed that Washington had passed the news on to the Marquis de Lafayette, who was then trying to hold the Continental Army together at Valley Forge. Surely, the Frenchman had learned "Mr. Burgoyne is destined to pass the present Winter in Massachusetts." Anticipating "the Criticism of all the politicians in the Civilized World," he now sought "to have the approbation of those in our own Country." He informed Lafayette that Burgoyne had not negotiated honestly since the surrender. Indeed, Laurens had no doubt that the British general "will appear to have been the dupe of his own policy." Still, uncertainty remained. "If in this we have acted wisely," he concluded, "it will be set to our Credit in opposition to some of our supposed errors."[26] Laurens never identified the mysterious critics, nor does it seem that Lafayette responded. Nor did the famed German drill master Baron de Kalb. Laurens wrote to him, "If I do not ask too much let me intreat your sentiments—will the Courts in Europe acknowledge our Act to be founded in Justice & good policy?"[27] He even requested his son John, a Continental officer, to "tell me your thoughts on our determination to suspend the embarkation of Mr. Burgoyne."[28]

Whatever answers Laurens received, revolutionary events moved on. In February, Congress learned France had recognized the independence of the United States, less an affirmation of republican government in America than a jab at its perennial enemy Great Britain. Laurens went on to serve the country's diplomatic interests. But the Burgoyne matter got under his skin. He kept replaying the debate at York. Had the United States done the right thing? At the end of the war—after Lord North had resigned as first minister—Laurens drafted a memo about the Burgoyne controversy. It is not clear why he did so—other than that he thought the basic issues had never been properly resolved. He reviewed once again the surrender of arms at Saratoga, the lack of quality housing at Cambridge, and the possibility that the Convention Army might have joined General Howe in New York City. Congress was especially concerned with the military risk. "Had the Convention Troops reached New York or Philadelphia, they would instantly have been employed against us," he assured himself in 1782. "Congress might have clamored, but their complaints would have been treated as former complaints had been, with contempt. And the World at large would have laughed at them."[29]

News that the Congress canceled the departure of the British army reached Burgoyne early in 1778. It was a crushing blow. His health was not good. But more pressing were the reports from London that his enemies were attacking his reputation. He desperately sought an audience with George III so that he could explain the surrender of six thousand troops. Now he was trapped. As Laurens remembered, "When General Burgoyne found the ill effect of his Letter [about the breach of faith], his temper sowered [soured], he became crabbed & sought for occasions to pick quarrels with the American Military."[30] His behavior was even worse. Burgoyne lashed out at an American colonel—David Henley—and triggered a court-martial that dramatically devolved into a contest over the meaning of honor.

• CHAPTER 6 •

American at the Bar

Colonel David Henley's ordeal began on January 20, 1778. His trial for engaging in dishonorable conduct as a Continental officer was held in a small Cambridge courthouse. The presentation of evidence lasted almost a month, punctuated occasionally by adjournments for heavy snow and the illness of the prosecutor, who happened to be General Burgoyne, then a British prisoner trapped in the United States.

On most days the building was overflowing, drawing a diverse crowd of prisoners, American officers, and people living in the community. A German soldier informed a friend back home, "The chief amusement we have at present is a suit between General Burgoyne and an American colonel named Henley." He was especially surprised to discover that ordinary people were welcome. As he reported, "Every male person can attend such a court and everyone is permitted to take notes. The court-house is packed, and not even the humblest is refused admittance."[1]

Spectators often braved heavy snow to witness the proceedings. Just getting there was a real challenge. One man who challenged the elements noted, "The whole winter has almost been one storm. The winds are so violent and accompanied by such mighty blasts that the wooden houses fairly shake and tremble."[2] Some people

A North-Easterly Perspective View of Cambridge Court House, Robert Hallowell [Gardiner]. (Harvard University Archives, HUC 8782.514 [82])

simply wanted to catch sight of Major General John Burgoyne, an audacious showman who did his best to dominate the proceedings. Others lent support for Henley, an officer from nearby Charlestown who had achieved an impressive war record. Whatever their motives, everyone—the British as well as the Americans—understood the trial involved a lot more than passing entertainment or expressions of loyalty for a respected revolutionary.

At stake throughout the proceedings was a new republic's capability for delivering justice. The trial unexpectedly exposed the burden of independence. Could the United States handle separation from Great Britain responsibly? The Americans eagerly wanted to demonstrate that they could do so; the British were skeptical. The questions raised at the trial were similar to those that had provoked a troubled congressional debate at York. But in this intimate environment, abstract issues about honor and reputation became personal. Burgoyne brilliantly exploited American insecurity, asking the court repeatedly, Was the United States civilized enough to enjoy the world's respect?—which in his mind, of course, meant British approval.

The defensiveness of American officials during the entire contest resulted in a series of extraordinary concessions. As we shall learn, they gave way to Burgoyne on almost every point. It seemed at times as if the ongoing Revolution was only a remote consideration. General Heath and other officers who had just negotiated Burgoyne's surrender at Saratoga allowed the British general—after all, a prisoner of war—to control the court-martial of an American soldier.

* * *

From the start, events in the courtroom defied normal expectations. After all, General Burgoyne focused his frustration and wrath on an extraordinarily unpromising target. Since the American raid on British sniper posts had interrupted a performance of Burgoyne's play in Boston, David Henley had risen rapidly in the ranks of the Continental Army, becoming a major in his twenties and then, after only a year, a full colonel. He enjoyed the backing of General Heath, who early in the war recognized Henley's talent as a field officer. It also helped that Henley came from a well-established merchant-farmer family in Charlestown. Although nothing is known about Henley's education, he was identified on some documents as "esquire," an indication of solid social standing.

David Henley (1749–1823). (Tennessee Virtual Archive)

Before becoming commander of the prisoner-of-war camp in Cambridge, Henley had already achieved a distinguished military record. During George Washington's chaotic retreat from New York City in late 1777, Henley earned the praise of superior officers. They were impressed by his ability to recruit and command new units. When reports circulated that Henley deserved greater responsibilities, Washington intervened immediately, explaining to the Massachusetts Board of War that he had "order'd Colo. Henly on to Camp, with a View of providing for Him in Some other Capacity. I consider Him as too valuable An Officer to permit Him to be lost to the Service." He instructed Henley to raise a new regiment "with all diligence and dispatch" and urged Massachusetts authorities to provide Henley with "every kind of Countenance and assistance which his merit and the good of the service demand."[3] William Tudor, who would later defend Henley at the court-martial, offered even more enthusiastic testimony. He informed John Adams that Henley was one of "the 3 best Majors we have in the Army. They are spirited and sensible and have taken great Pains with their respective Regiments."[4] Curiously, the only qualified assessment came from Henley's patron Heath, who described him as "a brave and good officer, but warm and quick in his natural temper"—the very attribute that brought him to the bar.[5]

Although it is hard to judge the impact of grief on anyone, it seems plausible that Henley's irascibility may have resulted from the recent loss of his younger brother. Thomas Henley enthusiastically supported American independence. While he was studying in London—an indication that the family was prosperous—he learned that New Englanders had resisted the British army at Lexington and Concord. He immediately returned to Massachusetts, where he joined a new regiment. His intelligence and commitment soon attracted the attention of General Heath, who, during the ill-fated New York campaign to keep General Howe from occupying New York City, appointed Thomas his aide-de-camp. By that time, Thomas had become the youngest major in the Continental Army.

Then, just as his career was taking off, Thomas Henley was killed in action. On September 23, 1776, perhaps acting on faulty information, Heath ordered a raid on Montresor's Island (now Randall's Island in the East River). Henley begged repeatedly to join the assault on the British position. At first, Heath refused the request, reminding Henley that a staff officer properly should remain at headquarters. Henley persisted. Nothing went according to plan. Not only were the British defenders prepared to meet the attack, but also several American officers were clearly guilty of cowardice under fire—behavior that resulted in courts-martial. Henley died trying to help a wounded American officer during a chaotic retreat. The news of Thomas's death came as a crushing blow to Washington. He issued a General Order announcing, "Major Henly Aid-de-Camp to Genl Heath, whose Activity and Attention to duty, Courage and every other Quality, which can distinguish a brave and gallant Soldier, must endear him to every Lover of his Country, [has] fallen in a late Skirmish on Montresor's Island while bravely leading a party on."[6] David organized his brother's funeral, a sad and painful moment, one that may help explain his tetchy response to disorder and insolence among the British prisoners on Prospect Hill.

David Henley never asked to oversee the prison camp—at least, there is no record of him having done so. The assignment signaled Heath's trust in the man. Still, Henley must have known that this was no ordinary assignment. Control of six thousand unhappy soldiers required unquestioned obedience to his own authority, patience when challenged, and genuine concern for the needs of prisoners and residents. The New York campaign had not prepared him for this moment. Mercy Otis Warren, an astute observer, assessed the delicate situation: "This idle dissipated army, lay too long in the neighborhood of Boston, for the advantage of either side." Cold, bored, and anxious to return home, Burgoyne's soldiers posed a threat to civil society. According to Warren, "They corrupted the students of Harvard college, and the youth of the capital and its environs, who were allured to enter into their gambling parties, and other scenes of licentiousness. They became acquainted with the designs, the resources, and the weaknesses of America; and there were many among them, whose talents and captivity rendered them capable of making the most mischievous use of their knowledge."[7]

The incidents triggering the crisis initially seemed relatively minor. Maintaining order in the camp was a daily problem. The British forged passes allowing them unauthorized contact with townspeople; they obtained large quantities of liquor. Such misconduct was routine, and the American guards—often assisted by British officers—dealt with them as well as might be expected. But Burgoyne seized on two exchanges, accusing Henley of a pathological hatred of the British that put the entire Convention Army in danger of massacre. The charges of mental instability were so hyperbolic that they struck people who attended the trial as incredible, even risible. Still, Burgoyne insisted on registering his complaints, and as with any complex legal action, resolution turned on the interpretation of facts and the integrity of witnesses.

The first challenge to Henley's authority occurred on December 16, 1777. He ordered a group of British prisoners accused of violating prison regulations to turn out in front of a barrack for review. It was a routine request. Henley was mounted on a horse. He asked each soldier what he had done, and since most infractions were minor, Henley dismissed them. That is, all of them except for Corporal Reeves. His transgression involved an unauthorized visit to town where he had insulted an American officer. Reeves may have been drinking. He told Henley that he was sorry for his behavior. Moreover, if he had known he had disparaged an American officer, he would not have behaved so rudely. After Henley heard the story, he was not inclined to overlook the offense. Sensing more trouble, Reeves began yelling, insisting that he was a good soldier and wanted to fight for his king. Henley repeatedly demanded silence, perhaps fearing other prisoners might support Reeves.

At that moment, Henley dismounted. He requested an American guard to give him a firelock with an attached bayonet. Again, he insisted on silence. Reeves, who may still have been drunk, ignored the command. Henley approached the British soldier, and slightly wounded the man with the bayonet. He may have contemplated a second thrust, but another British prisoner standing next to Reeves deflected the weapon. Reeves returned to the barracks, shouting insults. A doctor treated him and reported the injury amounted to little more than a scratch. And with that assessment the confrontation ended. Henley does not seem to have been particularly worried about what had occurred. No one came forward with accusations of misbehavior—nothing was said until Burgoyne later announced that a brave British soldier had been martyred by an avenging American officer.

The basic facts, however, invited dispute. The court-martial raised questions about Henley's state of mind. Why did he dismount, for example? Could he not have issued orders more effectively from the horse? Was he intent on violence? Or was he merely attempting to bring order to a situation that might have encouraged other disgruntled prisoners to support Reeves? Did Henley's timely action head off a riot? And then, there was the weapon. Why did Henley demand a firelock? Was the bayonet thrust meant simply as a warning to a disruptive solider, or did Henley intend to kill Reeves? Would he have done so had another British prisoner not intervened?

The second incident dominating Henley's trial occurred on January 9. Reports about what exactly happened were confused, often contradictory. The basic narrative mentions an attack on a lone American sentry the previous day. Something he said angered a group of British prisoners, and they not only assaulted him but also stole his firelock. The American was badly injured. Anxious to arrest the soldier allegedly responsible for the beating and return the weapon, Henley ordered a company of armed American guards to conduct a search of one of the barracks. About a hundred troops marched from Winter Hill to Prospect Hill. When they arrived, a large group of ill-tempered British prisoners was milling about. When Henley commanded them to make way for his men, they resisted, moving very slowly, mumbling insults, and crowding in very close to the file of guards. Several Americans felt threatened, and while pushing disruptive British soldiers out of the path, they stabbed two of them. The wounds were not serious. Henley had not given a command for what appeared to be spontaneous defensive acts. Indeed, he was standing several yards away from the encounter. Order was quickly reestablished, and a thorough search of British quarters failed to recover the missing weapon. Henley ordered the arrest of eighteen British soldiers who had obstructed the Americans. That was not all. Henley himself stabbed a recalcitrant soldier who moved off the field too slowly. Again, the wound did not threaten the man's life.

During the trial, Burgoyne held Henley personally responsible for the entire melee. If he had maintained control over his own men during a tense confrontation, Burgoyne claimed, Henley could have stopped the violence against innocent bystanders. At issue was not confusion during the march nor the actions of excitable American guards. Rather, Burgoyne insisted that Henley's profound hatred of the British prisoners had poisoned the atmosphere of the camp, and by communicating his contempt to his own men, he encouraged them to behave in a criminal manner. Of course, the Americans dismissed this argument out of hand. Considering the beating of the sentry, the theft of a weapon, and the surly mood of the British prisoners, it was striking a riot had been avoided.

* * *

The precise moment when Burgoyne learned he would not be able to return to England when he had planned is not known. In early January he must have suspected that something had gone very wrong, and he would not be allowed to leave. The collapse of the Convention agreement left him angry and depressed. He complained of ill-health. More important for him was his inability to defend his reputation before the king and Parliament.

As the winter closed in, he became increasingly desperate, allowing frustration to fuel episodes of foul temper. As Henry Laurens later reported, Burgoyne seriously miscalculated the impact of his letter claiming the Americans had acted in bad faith. George Washington, who was trying to hold his army together at Valley Forge, warned that as a result of his despair, Burgoyne might stage a breakout. He instructed Heath to increase the strength of the prison guards.

Burgoyne probably should have resisted the temptation to write letters when he was angry. His protest about inadequate housing in Cambridge that set off a critical congressional debate served as a warning, but on January 9, sensing that the Convention Army would not soon depart for England, he gave free rein to ill-temper—the very weakness he denounced in Henley.

Reports of the disturbance on Prospect Hill provided Burgoyne with all the justification he needed. Writing to Heath, he explained that although the British prisoners had endured "provocations from your people . . . of the most atrocious nature," he had been willing to let the Americans deal with the incidents. However, Henley's actions were too serious to ignore. The arrest of several British soldiers after the disturbance before the barracks could not be tolerated. He insisted that Heath apologize for what had happened.[8]

Burgoyne could have ended the letter at that point. He pushed on, however, recounting a history of "insults and provocations" that the British had suffered in Cambridge. These incidents, which he did not describe, were so revolting that they dishonored the American military. The guards knew of these horrendous events, but "with haughtiness, sometimes with derision" they failed to address the situation. How could such criminal indifference be explained? The person responsible was none other than Colonel Henley, whose "language and conduct . . . encourages his inferiors, and seems calculated to excite the most bloody purposes." This "evil" pattern had to stop, and an indignant Burgoyne informed Heath he expected more than an apology. He wanted the Americans to punish Henley "for behavior heinously criminal as an officer, and unbecoming a man, [and for] the most indecent, violent, vindictive severity against unarmed men and of intentional murder." Without further explanation, Burgoyne assumed that Heath—an honorable officer—would schedule "a proper tribunal." When that moment of reckoning arrived, Burgoyne promised, "I will take care that undeniable evidence shall be produced to support these charges."[9]

Burgoyne's extraordinary demand surprised and annoyed Heath. In his response, he insisted that he had no information about the alleged provocations. He promised to look into the matter, assuring Burgoyne that the Americans organized the prison camps "on the principles of honour, reason, and justice." Moreover, the British were responsible for many clashes. There was a long chronicle of their harassing the guards. "Sentries have been repeatedly insulted on their Posts, & sometimes beat & disarmed," he wrote. These assaults reflect "Dishonor on themselves [the prisoners] for a Sentry is never to allow himself to be insulted or abused."[10]

Burgoyne's letter raised another sensitive point for Heath. Apparently, he had asserted—as he had done during the first dinner with Heath in Boston—that only British officers should punish British soldiers who broke camp rules. Even to suggest such a policy insulted the American general. Whatever Burgoyne might think, the British were prisoners of war, not parolees possessing special rights and privileges. On this topic, there could be no confusion. He and the American officers oversaw all aspects of prison life, including criminal actions. "I have been informed of late," Heath declared in a sharp retort to Burgoyne, "that some have hinted that such of your troops as break my orders, ought to be tried and punished by your orders. Even to mention of such a thing, I conceive to be (to use your own words in a late letter, with a little variation) a sort of insult that a man of military erudition in any country would be ashamed of, as being repugnant to every idea of military discipline."[11] The farmer from Roxbury was not about to accept a lecture on proper conduct from a British aristocrat.

At this point one might have expected Heath to conclude his letter to Burgoyne. He had asserted his own authority in no uncertain terms. But then, in a totally unexpected turnaround, Heath announced that he had ordered Henley's immediate arrest and had empaneled a military court of inquiry under Brigadier General Glover to examine the charges brought against the American colonel. Why Heath would make such a stunning concession to Burgoyne is hard to explain. He had no special training in military law. Heath seems to have been sensitive to public opinion, but that claim begs the question, What could public opinion have meant in this context? Did concern over the reaction of other American leaders or the heads of European governments—even Great Britain's—persuade Heath to appease Burgoyne? In his *Memoir* published several decades later, he maintained his original goal had been defending "the honour of the United States."[12] There is no reason to doubt his sincerity. The challenge for both generals was accepting the other man's definition of honor.

Before the legal proceedings began, Burgoyne offered Heath a bizarre proposition, which if nothing else revealed just how poorly he interpreted the character of his adversaries. In another impulsive note he managed to turn the negotiations over the Henley trial into a bitter personal matter. His tone was condescending and insulting. Burgoyne suggested that the major reason for Heath's original skepticism about the criminal behavior of the American guards was his reliance on biased evidence. The source of the misinformation was none other than Henley, a prejudiced officer who had misled the naïve Heath. There were other culprits. Indeed, Burgoyne warned his American counterpart of a vast conspiracy determined to deny the British justice. "Cambridge and Boston abound with ill-designing Men who propagate calumny in order to color persecution," Burgoyne explained. "The whole Air is contaminated with lies—Beware, Sir, of such reporters—They are your Enemies as well as mine—they strike at the character of your state." Trying to curry favor with Heath was surely a nonstarter. Burgoyne added an insulting taunt, claiming, "I offer proof of grievance, you recriminate upon hearsay"—a curious comment considering Heath had just authorized a formal investigation into the charges against Henley.[13]

Burgoyne's inept attempt to insert himself in domestic politics backfired. Heath would have none of it. He had reliable intelligence about the people in the area who posed a potential threat to his authority. "If Cambridge and Boston abound with ill-designing Men," Heath informed Burgoyne, "I hope I shall be able to distinguish my Enemies." Burgoyne's misstep may have resulted from his own experience in England—where rival generals and treacherous members of Parliament defamed rivals to advance their own careers. Heath was ambitious, but he refused to turn the Henley affair into a personal matter. He cared more about his country's reputation than his own. What had been Burgoyne's motive in warning the American commander? Certainly, it was not a declaration of universal camaraderie among senior military officers. "I can scarcely believe that one who is frequently bestowing invectives either on my Country, its Laws, Officers or Inhabitants (I need not say myself) can be a friend," Heath wrote. "And I wish you, Sir, carefully to avoid such expressions in your letters, unless you mean to give offense."[14]

Heath moved ahead with the investigation of Henley. The general was determined to follow established procedure according to the military code. That decision meant he appointed General Glover to be the president of a court of inquiry, which, in a way much like a grand jury in civil cases, examined the charges, interviewed witnesses, and determined whether to authorize a general court-martial. Perhaps still irritated by Burgoyne's remark that Heath relied only on hearsay whereas the British general had real proof, Heath declared the court of inquiry would be "founded on more than hearsay."[15]

Assurance of fairness failed to satisfy Burgoyne. He suspected the court of inquiry was simply a furtive attempt by the Americans to postpone judgment. In another intemperate note, Burgoyne informed Heath that "the slight and indifferent manner in which you take up [a] matter of such magnitude makes me apprehensive." He concluded the Americans were playing him. Can you "seriously mean to put me off by a Court of Inquiry, in which neither the judges nor the witnesses are under the Obligation of an oath?" he asked. There was no need for a preliminary investigation. Burgoyne pleaded, "A Court of Inquiry if I have any understanding of so plain and expressive a term is applicable only in cases of doubt & suspicion."[16] He had no question about Henley's guilt. In his opinion the purpose of a general court-martial was not to give the accused a chance to prove his innocence but, rather, to demonstrate his guilt.

Speed was vital, since Burgoyne feared that as news of Henley's situation spread among the American guards, no British prisoner would be safe. After all, he argued, slowly developing legal procedures—the court of inquiry in particular—tended "to excite Men to horrid and extensive massacre of those whom it is their duty to guard." Although the danger to the prisoners was more imagined than real, Burgoyne lectured Heath: The Convention Army should not be exposed to violence. Did Heath really want to take the risk? "By the universal Law of Nations," Burgoyne railed, "we have a right to personal protection, among generous ones we should have found hospitality—Upon this right, and in the Name of the State of Great Britain, I protest against the Court of Inquiry . . . and demand a Court Martial properly constituted for criminal jurisdiction in cases of the most atrocious nature to pass judgment upon the conduct of Colonel Henley."[17]

Heath held his ground. To be sure, the members of the court of inquiry were not required to take an oath, nor were the witnesses sworn. Burgoyne would just have to accept those conditions. After all, as Heath reminded Burgoyne, these rules were the "Custom of the American Army."[18] On this point Heath was probably misinformed. In a book published in New York only a few years earlier, a British officer explained, "The place of a Grand Jury is supplied by a Court of Inquiry, which is often held, previous to a Court Martial, where there is a doubt of sufficiency of cause to bring an offender before that Judicature."[19] Nevertheless, Heath was not about to take a history lesson from Burgoyne. "Although you may view a Court of Inquiry as inadequate, dilatory, and nugatory," he observed, "it has been the first step commonly taken in our army."[20]

Heath told Burgoyne not to worry about being massacred along with his soldiers. They would all receive "personal protection." Such considerate treatment was more than the American prisoners had experienced in the floating coffins in New York Harbor. Heath informed Burgoyne that "as much generosity and hospitality may be found in my country as in any, and I will add more than in some others, if we may judge from the treatment of the unfortunate."[21]

The court of inquiry met on January 18 and quickly issued its findings. After reviewing the charges brought by Burgoyne against Henley—and taking them under "mature consideration"—the military panel headed by President Glover decided "from the evidence offered on the side of General Burgoyne, against Col. Henley, it will be more to the honor of Col. Henley, as well as for the satisfaction of all interested that the judgment of a Court Martial should be taken on his conduct during his command at Cambridge."[22]

The charge which Burgoyne had originally stated ten days earlier remained the focus of the trial. Henley would be tried at a "special General Court Martial" for the "general tenor of language and conduct heinously criminal as an officer, and unbecoming a man, of the most indecent, violent, vindictive severity against unarmed men, and of intentional murder."[23] Astonishingly, the court of inquiry had endorsed the complaint of a prisoner of war. Everything seemed to be going Burgoyne's way. He might, however, have noted more closely the court's concern for preserving the honor of Colonel Henley.

* * *

General Heath's initial concession to Burgoyne raised annoying new problems testing the country's resolve to deliver justice in very hard cases. Heath was, of course, thoroughly familiar with how courts-martial were supposed to work. He had ordered several military trials during the New York campaign. These events generally dealt with predictable offenses such as desertion, failure to obey commands, and petty theft—all covered by the Articles of War.

The Cambridge trial promised to be much more complex. Burgoyne's aggressive intervention presented an obvious difficulty. So, too, did the law itself. The rules governing miliary behavior traced their origins back more than a century to Great Britain. The procedures governing Henley's tribunal were borrowed from English experience and then, because there was a revolution in progress, reframed in America so they seemed distinctly different from those of the former imperial regime. The challenge proved extremely difficult. As the entire confrontation with Burgoyne would reveal—often with some embarrassment for the Americans—the Articles of War were part of a broad cultural heritage that governed expectations and practices long after Americans declared political independence.

Where could Heath turn at this moment? We can assume that a copy of Stephen Payne Adye's influential *Treatise on Courts Martial* found its way into his personal library. It was a popular reference book first published in New York in 1769 and subsequently republished in London. Indeed, the title is still in print. Adye served in America as an artillery officer in the British army, and during the 1760s, he became fascinated with the practical aspects of military law. With obvious pride, he introduced the work: "No Author, I believe, has ever wrote on Courts Martial before, though something on that Subject was much wanting for the Guidance of Officers, who may be employed on that Duty; therefore, if this Treatise had no other Merit, it may certainly claim that of being new."[24] Among other topics, it contained an exhaustive description of the role of the judge advocate in courts-martial.

At a time when many colonial Americans claimed to be repelled by how brutally the British punished soldiers—often a hundred lashes for seemingly minor offenses—Adye offered a more humane view of military punishment. "The laws of Man," he noted, "are supposed to be founded on the laws of God and nature, but to observe strictly that of Retaliation or the *lex talionis,* which is, Eye for Eye, wound for wound, stripe for stripe, &c. would not suit the present degenerate age." Burgoyne may have missed this passage. Although Adye did not provide specific advice about dealing with an officer accused of "intentional murder," he did counsel judge advocates to "make it appear that a detestation of the crime, and a regard to the public safety, are not inconsistent with pity to the man; particularly to offenders for the first crime, to such whose crimes are small, whose temptations were powerful and who appear to have been seduced by others."[25]

Another, more recent code was available. The provincial government of Massachusetts recognized the need to establish discipline in its army well before the Battle of Bunker Hill. The military consisted largely of local militia units. The troops brought enthusiasm and courage to the fight, but they had their own ideas about the rules for active service. When George Washington first arrived in Massachusetts in July 1776, for example, he encountered independent companies lacking "proper Discipline & Subordination." He diplomatically explained the situation: "This unhappy & devoted Province has been so long in a State of Anarchy, & the Yoke of ministerial Oppression has been so heavily laid on it that great Allowances are to be made for Troops raised under such Circumstances."[26]

Aware of the pressing need to transform patriotic farmers into reliable soldiers, the state passed the "Rules and Articles for the better government of the Troops," and while the document borrowed heavily from English army regulations, it emphatically insisted that Massachusetts was no longer a British colony. In words that Heath and other people who traced their genealogies back to the Puritan founders would have endorsed, the Articles of War recounted—in oddly nostalgic terms—almost two hundred years of regional history:

> Whereas the lust of power which of old oppressed, persecuted and exiled our pious and virtuous ancestors from their possessions in Britain, now pursues with tenfold severity us, their guileless children, who are unjustly and wickedly charged with licentiousness, sedition, treason, and rebellion . . . do think it our indispensable duty, by all lawful ways and means in our power, to recover, maintain, defend, and preserve the free exercise of all those civil and religious rights and liberties, for which our forefathers fought, bled and died.[27]

The Provincial Congress predicted that the inhabitants of Massachusetts would "cheerfully" obey "Officers chosen by themselves," and avoid "cruel punishments as are usually practiced in Standing Armies." These were rules for a genuinely American force, one straining to distinguish itself from the British army, one founded "in reason, honour and virtue."[28] We know the judge advocate for the Henley trial owned one of the few surviving copies of the *Rules and Regulations.* It addressed mutiny, desertion, and disrespect for officers, but not surprisingly, it provided little guidance for dealing with the histrionic charges brought by Burgoyne.

Confronted with a real war, the Continental Congress decided that the Massachusetts code needed to be reframed to reflect the interests of the entire nation. Ironically, the representatives devised nationally sanctioned articles of war that conformed more closely with British precedent. However, they knew it was not acceptable simply to copy those regulations, and without recounting the long history of the colonies since the first Puritans arrived, Congress provided a preamble providing a general explanation of why colonial Americans had been forced to rebel against the king.

Congress placed the blame directly on George III. After all, "His Majesty's most faithful subjects in these Colonies are reduced to a dangerous and critical situation, by the attempts of the British

Ministry, to carry into execution, by force of arms, several unconstitutional and oppressive acts of the British parliament for laying taxes in America, to enforce the collection of these taxes, and for altering and changing the constitution and internal police of some of these Colonies, in violation of the natural and civil rights of the Colonies."[29]

The national military "Rules and Orders" contain sixty-nine articles. As one would expect, most of them describe predictable offenses and how senior officers should deal with them. Only two seem relevant to Henley's ordeal. The precise wording is significant for understanding how events unfolded at Cambridge. Article 47 states: "Whatsoever commissioned officer shall be convicted before a general court-martial, of behaving in a scandalous, infamous manner, such as is unbecoming the character of an officer and a gentleman, shall be discharged from the service."[30]

As with all general legal language of this sort, the challenge for prosecutors and jury at Cambridge was defining in a specific and very unusual context, the interpretation of words. What, in fact, constituted scandalous behavior? How was a gentleman supposed to act? Was "gentleman" defined in British terms or from a very different cultural perspective in America? Did the expression refer to one's social status or to a vague set of principles to which any decent person might be expected to subscribe? Could an infamous officer still be a gentleman, or were the two categories overlapping?

The best guide through this interpretive thicket remains William Winthrop, judge advocate general after the Civil War, whose *Military Law and Precedents* (1896) provides an impressively detailed analysis of the American Articles of War, which were in force during the Revolution. As for providing an appropriate guide on these matters, there is no question. He was called by some the William Blackstone of his field, since like the great eighteenth-century jurist who provided a brilliant commentary on the common law, he produced the definitive survey of military law. Winthrop did not downplay the complex issues that roiled the Henley trial. Concentrating on

Article 47—the most relevant section—he explains how the officers at a court-martial should view the word "unbecoming." It is understood, Winthrop advised, "to mean not merely inappropriate or unsuitable, as being opposed to good taste or propriety or not consonant with usage, but morally unbefitting and unworthy."[31] In other words, a one-off error of judgment—no matter how vulgar—did not meet the legal standard.

The word "gentleman" proved harder to explain. It carried both moral and social implications. According to Winthrop: "This term is believed to be used, not simply to designate a person of education, refinement and good breeding and manners, but to indicate such a gentleman as an officer of the army is expected to be, viz. a man of honor; that is to say, a man of a high sense of justice, of an elevated standard of morals and manners, and of corresponding general deportment." Winthrop noted that judges should weigh what constituted acts "unbecoming" for an officer and for a "gentleman" as separate elements, since behavior that seemed unbecoming for an officer might not be so for a gentleman.

Confronted with such puzzling advice, we might ask, What practical direction could a person such a Heath, one not formally trained in military law, have taken from Article 47? Winthrop had an answer. An act deemed unbecoming for a gentleman and officer "must offend so seriously against law, justice, morality or decorum as to expose to disgrace, socially or as a man, the offender, and at the same time must be of such a nature or committed under such circumstances as to bring dishonor or disrepute upon the military profession which he represents."[32] The specific charges against Henley—"indecent, violent, vindictive severity . . . and intentional murder"—seemed to meet the law's requirement—at least, they did for Burgoyne.

• CHAPTER 7 •

Enemy for the Prosecution

General Burgoyne transformed a Cambridge courtroom into a legal stage. Striding into the small building each day, week after week, he commanded attention—from his own soldiers and from American revolutionaries. Clever, charming, and focused, he presented himself during the Henley trial as a kind of celebrity figure common today, but with the exception of some evangelical preachers, it was rare to encounter such a charismatic figure in eighteenth-century public life. Burgoyne created his own beguiling script in which he played the lead. In this production, a British prisoner of war in America announced he represented the "opinion of mankind."[1]

* * *

What do we actually know about the details of the trial? The surviving records were the product of an intense contest between strong-willed military figures and the countries for which they were fighting. It is no surprise that the rivalry in the Cambridge courthouse generated several competing print narratives of the court-martial. They all claimed to offer a definitive story. The battle of texts began in Massachusetts. On June 1, 1778, more than a month after the conclusion of the trial, John Gill, a Boston printer described at the time as "a sound Whig"—in other words, as a reliable supporter of independence—announced the release of "The Proceedings of a General Court-Martial, Held at Cambridge."[2] The publication ran eighty-eight pages, an impressive length since during wartime the raw materials needed to make paper were scarce. Printers often appealed to the public for rags and cloth just to stay in business. That scarcity explains why the number of new titles issued in the United States immediately after independence dropped dramatically. More significant, Gill listed the price as twelve shillings, an outlay that represented a real sacrifice for most people. Such challenges did not discourage Gill, who correctly assumed the work would be in high demand.

In an advertisement in the *Boston Gazette,* Gill aggressively marketed the product, informing readers of the newspaper, "As this Trial was a matter of much conversation last winter—the Printer presumes the Public will not be displeased at now having it in their power to read the Speeches of the Extraordinary Personage [Burgoyne] who makes a principal figure in it, and in what manner this Loyal General could address a number of men whom his Master would call a Rebel Court-Martial." The announcement appeared in at least two other Boston journals.[3]

The text itself gives the impression of being the actual transcript of the entire trial. It was not, in fact, an official court record. Gill never provided the source of the document, which contained not only long legal arguments but also the detailed testimony of a score of British and American soldiers called as witnesses. There was a possibility that Gill himself modified the text. Even at the time, it was hard to distinguish fact from rumor. A German prisoner complained, "We can obtain no reliable information from the vicinity, and I have made up my mind to believe nothing I hear. The number of lies that are printed and carried from mouth to mouth is almost beyond belief."[4]

The issue of textual evidence became more puzzling when a few months later a prominent London publisher, John Almon (1737–1805), began selling a booklet bearing the title *Proceedings of a*

Court-Martial, Held at Cambridge. This version was over a hundred pages long. Much of Gill's Boston text—especially the interrogation of British and American soldiers—is repeated in the London document, and historians have assumed that Almon simply pirated Gill's work.

That was not the case—at least, not entirely. The difference should have been obvious from Almon's title page. Unlike the Boston version, it informs English readers that they will learn how Burgoyne accused Henley "of ill treatment of the BRITISH SOLDIERS." And it identifies a source. The record owed its existence to notes "Taken in Short Hand by an Officer, who was present."[5] That handwritten record has not survived. What seems to have happened is that after the disgraced Burgoyne returned to England in April 1778, he gave Almon a copy of Gill's title, and working together, they edited the Boston text so that Burgoyne's speeches are fuller and the American judge advocate's arguments and summation reduced.

A third account survives. Burgoyne was so eager to control the flow of information about Henley's trial that he authorized a short publication giving prominence to his own dramatic speeches at Cambridge. Just as he was leaving the United States for the final time, he commissioned John Howe, a loyalist printer who had recently fled Boston and established a press in Newport, Rhode Island, to run off copies. The city was then occupied by the British army. The highly one-sided account contained only nineteen pages. It was published as *Substance of General Burgoyne's Speeches at a Court-Martial held at Cambridge.*[6] If nothing else, the collection of Burgoyne's court speeches revealed how much Henley had gotten under the general's skin. It also suggests that Burgoyne had written out his presentations in advance, in other words, not as spontaneous arguments but like monologues in a play, texts carefully crafted for dramatic impact.

Instead of compromising the value of the competing transcripts—after all, what counts as testimony is always subject to interpretation—the textual discrepancies (most of them minor) serve to highlight the cultural differences informing the entire trial. Their clashing perspectives on the ability of a revolutionary regime to deliver justice invite us to sit with the military panel of thirteen Continental officers serving as the jury. They reached a unanimous verdict, one with which we might disagree. But personal culpability is not the main point of the story. The dueling accounts of what happened on Prospect Hill—together with newspaper accounts—remind us how a former colonial society struggled to comprehend the responsibilities of independence.

* * *

The general court-martial of Colonel David Henley began on Tuesday, January 20, 1778, at 10:00 a.m. After the first session, the trial settled into a routine. Every day General Burgoyne made a dramatic entrance followed by two senior generals who had served during the Saratoga campaign—Major General William Phillips and Major General Friedrich von Riedesel. They appeared as proud representatives of Great Britain, arriving each morning in full regimental uniform, figures of self-conscious theater.

Various staff officers who took notes and advised Burgoyne on points of law advised the generals. The group shared a large table with the American Judge Advocate William Tudor and his legal counselors. David Henley sat with the British and Americans. At the center of the room the president of the court-martial, Brigadier General John Glover had a chair as well as a lectern from which he occasionally spoke. Twelve American officers who served as the jurors were arranged on either side of the president.

A remarkable description of the layout of the courtroom has survived. A German prisoner witnessed the proceedings, which he noted with obvious disdain were "different from ours." He described the building "where a crowd of participants assembled each day" as oval, "having on all sides large church windows reaching to the roof." The central doors opened onto a single room. "The inside is nothing but a large hall," the spectator wrote, "the middle of which is partitioned off by a railing and two steps leading to a platform, thus making one half of the room one foot and a half higher than the other."[7] Glover sat opposite the door. The German did not mention heating—a real challenge during a hard winter—but in a packed room, he was able to hear clearly the testimony of the witnesses and the impassioned speeches of Burgoyne and Tudor.

Heath selected Glover to be president of the court. It was a prudent choice, since the general from nearby Marblehead had an excellent reputation as a hardworking, reliable Continental officer. After organizing the crossing of the Delaware River for Washington's troops, he became a local hero. More recently, Glover had accompanied Burgoyne on the long march from Saratoga to Cambridge, and he apparently felt comfortable later inviting the British general who was a prisoner on a personally supervised tour of several coastal towns north of Boston. He believed such a trip would demonstrate to Burgoyne the formidable population of the state and thus discourage the British from attacking the region.

Before approaching Burgoyne, Glover asked Heath for permission. Heath was skeptical, writing to George Washington that the expedition struck him as "rather impolitick, but General Glover is so importunate that I have told him that I would mention the matter to your Excellency."[8] Washington, who was always a step ahead of other American officers, rejected the idea out of hand. He informed Heath, "I think it would have been highly improper to have him [Burgoyne] allowed the liberty of visiting your Seaport Towns—A Man of his sagacity and penetration would make many observations upon situations &c. that might prove detrimental to us in future."[9] Washington understood that however much Burgoyne had overplayed his hand at Saratoga, and then at Cambridge, he remained a dangerous adversary.

Heath appointed William Tudor as judge advocate. Few other candidates for the post were as well prepared for the challenge as Tudor. A graduate of Harvard College in the class of 1769, he studied

William Tudor. (From *The Army Lawyer: A History of the Judge Advocate General's Corps, 1775–1975,* Wikimedia Commons)

law in the Boston office of John Adams. Tudor made a good impression on Adams, who repeatedly helped to advance the young man's career. Although Tudor initially had reservations about America's resistance to Great Britain—probably because he was madly in love with the daughter of a leading loyalist family—he joined the Continental Army. During the New York campaign, he served as a judge advocate under Heath's command, and by January 1777 he had risen to the rank of lieutenant colonel. While continuing his work as judge advocate, he was attached to a newly formed regiment under Colonel David Henley.[10]

No one at the time suggested that Tudor's friendship with Henley created a conflict of interest. After the war ended, some of his associates suggested that Tudor never quite fulfilled his early promise. They chided him for being lazy—a charge he would not have disputed—but when he appeared at Henley's court-martial, Tudor demonstrated extraordinary courtroom skills. He more than held his own against Burgoyne, revealing dramatically why John Adams described Tudor as having "a clear head and honest, faithful heart. He is virtuous, sober, steady, industrious, and constant in his office."[11] Not surprisingly, a British officer called Tudor "a little vain conceited fellow" who addressed the tribunal "in a pert flippant manner."[12]

Tudor did not take his duties lightly. He repeatedly demonstrated a thorough understanding of the responsibilities of the judge advocate. That officer, he knew, was the key figure in the court-martial. As Stephen Adye stated in *Treatise on Courts Martial,* the judge advocate "may be said to be the main spring of a Court Martial, for on him the Court depends for information concerning the legality as well as regularity of their conduct, and therefore if he errs, all may go wrong."[13]

The judge advocate had an obligation to inform the members of the court as well as the accused about the relevant articles of military code. Most officers, of course, were not trained in the details of the law. The judge advocate had, therefore, "to explain the points of law that may occur in the Course of their proceeding." He was expected to prosecute the case "in the name of the United States of America." Whatever his personal feelings about the allegations—he was supposed to remain "unprejudiced and neutral"—the judge advocate was not at liberty to change the formal charge as entered by the commanding officer, a curious element in the Henley trial since Heath entered a charge originally dictated by Burgoyne.[14]

The burden of office weighed heavily on Tudor. During complex trials such as the one at Cambridge, he was expected to maintain a difficult balance. On the one hand, he was the state's prosecutor. In that capacity, he called witnesses and entered objections when he deemed rulings by the court "inadmissible or objectionable." On the other hand, he counseled the accused about his rights. During the Henley trial, Tudor explained how he viewed these different responsibilities. "The Judge-Advocate," he observed, "acts in the double capacity of prosecutor and counsel to the prisoner, which, those who are acquainted with the proceedings of military courts, will allow not to be inconsistent duties."[15] The requirements of the office seemed straightforward. As Tudor soon discovered, however, this was not a normal court-martial.

Burgoyne insisted on a different set of rules based in large part on his interpretation of British tradition. No sooner had the participants gathered than he sprang an astonishing demand on the court, which caught Tudor by surprise. The British general informed Glover that he had no intention of sitting quietly as a spectator. He insisted on serving as a prosecutor and, in that capacity, to assist the American judge advocate. It was an audacious claim, made even more so since he remained throughout a prisoner of war. Burgoyne justified why he should help prosecute Henley before the entire court. First, he blamed Heath for the strange request. He reasoned that if Heath had handled the affair in the proper manner from the beginning—presumably by immediately punishing Henley—there would have been no need for a second prosecutor, certainly not a British one. After all, had the American general come forward earlier and "placed the court martial upon a more enlarged basis than the honor of an individual," Burgoyne would not have needed to insert himself in the proceedings.[16]

It is true that Heath conceded a lot to Burgoyne. But he did not share Burgoyne's desire to organize the court-martial on an enlarged basis—a fuzzy concept in any case. Burgoyne championed a larger vision, one that he assumed a parochial American might not fully understand. Heath's problem was that he insisted on focusing on personalities—on the alleged crime of one soldier—when he should have viewed the entire controversy as a matter of abstract justice. Burgoyne pointed out that if the Americans had treated the Convention Army from the beginning in a manner sanctioned by international law and justice—behaved in the way that a defeated army expected—the trial might have taken on an entirely different character.

And so, with a sense of aggrieved necessity, Burgoyne argued that British military tradition provided clear precedents for his actions. The fact that these examples came entirely from British experience in no way made them irrelevant for the immediate case. The Americans had recently been colonial subjects, after all. "This Country once allowed British precedent great weight in all their

Courts," Burgoyne lectured. "Whether the change in Government hath nullified the usages, as well as subverted the written positive institutions of England is left to the Court to determine."[17] The challenge was clear. Were revolutionary Americans prepared to take their place among the enlightened nations of the world? To help them, Burgoyne provided the court with a list of specific cases which he believed legitimated his self-appointment as prosecutor, all of them of doubtful relevance.

Tudor was incensed. He mounted a spirited counterargument. In his opinion, Burgoyne's intervention revealed a profound ignorance of military law—at least, as practiced in the United States. He urged the court to focus attention "on the customs which prevail in the American army and the supposed duty of the Judge Advocate." These elements were all that mattered in the current situation, not dramatic presentation, not theatrics. The language of Burgoyne's appeal—a distinctly English way of speaking that had swayed members of Parliament—had become a cultural weapon in Cambridge, a means to captivate recently liberated colonists still uncertain about the character of their own independence. He warned the jury not to be moved by histrionics. In any event, he argued that special pleadings were unnecessary, "except on a point of law, for which the Judge Advocate is presumed to be competent." Addressing the court, Tudor insisted, "I do not oppose these precedents because they are British; had they been from Portugal or Turkey, and been pertinent and reasonable, they ought to influence your determination."[18] He was a little disingenuous. It is doubtful that he or the court would have accepted Turkish rulings. The problem with the British examples was they were wrong—errors in law.

Tudor urged the court to concentrate on fundamentals. What, he asked, was the whole purpose of courts-martial? It seemed indisputable that the main justification for military trials was resolving disputes quickly, often for regiments on the march. Speed was essential. He believed it would be a mistake, therefore, to confuse military tribunals with courts of common law, where litigants "in a free society" were allowed rights "unknown in an army." As Tudor explained, "A man when he commences a soldier, makes temporary relinquishment of the privileges of a citizen." From this observation it followed logically that if the court allowed a second prosecutor to participate, it would undermine the need for a judge advocate. Indeed, it would create a dangerous precedent, since someone claiming to be a second prosecutor—as Burgoyne was doing—would force the regularly appointed judge advocate to rebalance his normal duties, essentially redefining himself principally as a defense attorney. As Tudor explained, "If a prosecutor (and in this case a very able one) is admitted in addition to the Judge Advocate, surely it would be unreasonable to deny counsel in defense of the prisoner—and then consider, Gentlemen, what would be the consequence: Every man brought before a Court Martial would be entitled to the same indulgence." Soldiers accused of crimes would demand a lawyer. And if that request was allowed, the practice would introduce into military tribunals "all the subtleties and delays which prevail in common law."[19]

The court ruled against Tudor. Its determination marked the second extraordinary concession to the British general—the first being the court-martial itself. But the Americans conceded even more. During the course of the trial, Burgoyne claimed—even though his standing as a special prosecutor had been contested—the right to comment on witness testimony. As an able trial lawyer, Tudor knew that a prosecutor—in this case the judge advocate—was expected to build a case through the accumulation of sworn evidence, and then, at the conclusion of the proceedings, to present a persuasive narrative of guilt drawing on testimony that was part of official record.

Burgoyne was determined to bend the rules. In his role as a self-appointed prosecutor, he demanded an independent voice. He insisted on presenting his own narrative, which of course clashed with the judge advocate's. Again, Tudor protested vehemently. According to the transcript of the trial, "The Judge Advocate took exception at General Burgoyne's claim to observe upon the evidence at the closing of the charge, and argued, that if the General was permitted to speak at all, it must be upon the principle of indulgence, and not of right."[20]

The court again ruled in Burgoyne's favor. After a discussion—presumably involving Glover and the members of the tribunal—it was decided that "General Burgoyne should have the liberty of remarking upon the evidence offered by Colonel Henley, and the Judge Advocate was directed to acquaint the General with this determination."[21] Heath apparently offered no objection. That was not surprising, since, as he had already demonstrated, he viewed Henley's trial as an opportunity to showcase the new nation's willingness to bend over backward to deliver justice, even if that meant allowing Burgoyne to flout normal procedure.

* * *

Henley rose from the center table, swore on a Bible to tell the truth, and responded to Burgoyne's charges, "not guilty." Throughout the trial he remained sullen, visibly annoyed that Heath had acceded to Burgoyne's complaints. As was his right, Henley occasionally asked the witnesses questions, but when the court later inquired whether he had anything specific to say about the charges, he responded enigmatically: "I have particular reasons, and in my own apprehension very sufficient, for declining to say a single word in answer to the illiberal abuse thrown upon me." In his opinion, the whole trial was unnecessary. After all, the entire procedure had no precedent. It was "a new thing under the sun."[22]

Under these circumstances Henley put his faith in the judge advocate. He expressed confidence that the members of the tribunal—as well as an "impartial public"—would acquit him of all charges.[23] Henley's belief that he enjoyed the support of public opinion deserves special attention. All the participants in this theatrical trial assumed they were performing before anonymous groups of spectators—in Henley's case, staunch revolutionaries in New England—who had their own ideas about honor and justice. In this narrative, Henley took pride in representing a newly independent nation.

Burgoyne was also intensely aware of the force of public opinion. He defined it differently, however. His intentions became clear during the first moments of the trial. He directed his opening remarks as self-appointed prosecutor at distant judges, the king and his ministers in London who blamed Burgoyne for an embarrassing defeat. Unlike Henley, Burgoyne had experience on the stage. The little Cambridge courthouse served as a theater, where he mounted a dramatic attack not only on Henley but also on the entire revolutionary regime.

Burgoyne announced he believed the Americans had in fact engaged in a general conspiracy to abuse the British prisoners. Such a sweeping charge, he confessed, would be hard to prove, and so he decided to focus his animus on a single Continental officer "upon the plain principle, that it was more candid to suppose one instigator of such evils than a general voluntary bad disposition among the American troops." It was not an argument designed to win over Glover or the Continental officers serving as jurors, but by airing the suspicion of unfairness, Burgoyne provided an excuse for a possible unfavorable verdict. The move also explained why he concentrated his interrogation of witnesses almost entirely on the "transactions of the 19th of December and the 8th of January."[24]

Burgoyne then laid out his strategy as prosecutor. He based his plan on what he called "the Principles upon which I act." These principles reflected personal values and were only loosely tied to the American Articles of War. First, Burgoyne stressed that the incidents on Prospect Hill were very serious, far more so than they might appear to someone ignorant of the actual evidence. He intended to demonstrate that "public faith has been shaken; wanton barbarities have been committed, and a general massacre of the troops under my care apparently threatened." For Burgoyne the severity of the situation raised the legal bar for judgment. What was at stake were crimes in which "the interests of human nature are concerned."[25]

It was a clever move. Henley's actions suddenly involved natural law. They raised abstract ethical standards more extensive than the interests of a single nation. A British officer, he insisted, would never engage in "vindictive personal resentment." Assuming the high moral ground, Burgoyne announced: "I stand upon broader and upon firmer Ground,—the Ground of natural Rights, personal Protection, and public Honour;—as I appeal to the great Principles and landmarks by which human Societies hold and are directed, and which whether in Times of Amity or Hostility, are held equally Sacred by the universal Concurrence of civilized Man."[26]

Burgoyne's two other guiding principles were more personal, even sentimental, in that they appealed to the American judges not as representatives of a legal system but as fellow soldiers. "A second inducement to appear here," he declared, "is that of private Honour. I have undertaken to accuse Colonel Henley in a degree that ought to affect the feelings of a soldier nearer than life."[27]

Burgoyne never questioned his own honor. Whether the American officers understood professional responsibility as he defined it would be revealed in the course of the trial. Even more poignant—certainly more theatrical—was Burgoyne's alleged bond between himself as a British general and the ordinary troops under his command. He claimed to speak for "the brave and honest British Soldier, a private Man, defenseless, because unarmed; ignorant of your Laws; unqualified to make good his Cause in a Court of Justice, has nowhere to look for Redress of Injury but his own Officers."[28] Since the American Articles of War were drawn almost completely from English codes, it is unlikely that ordinary British soldiers were ignorant of the law, but in an emotional monologue such details hardly mattered. One spectator—presumably a British prisoner—reported that Burgoyne's pitiful rhetoric reduced him to tears. On another occasion people in the court laughed at his excessive rhetoric. Burgoyne later complained of this behavior, insisting that they refused to admit the seriousness of Henley's crimes.[29]

Burgoyne's extraordinary opening statement contained a warning—really a threat—that seems surprisingly prescient in character. He viewed the printing and distribution of the trial transcript as a weapon, since once the record was widely available, the Americans would not be able to lie about what had happened on Prospect Hill or blame Burgoyne for a failure to mount an effective case against Henley. The world would judge. "You well know the whole of this Matter will be published, translated, considered, and commented upon by every Nation in the World," he lectured the court. The public review will not only document the "reality" of the contested event but also demonstrate what Burgoyne called the "perspicuity of Justice."[30] Glover may well have wondered what the British general meant. Burgoyne seems to have believed that civilized people wherever they might live wanted to learn more than the basic facts of the case. They demanded common sense and a demonstration of fairness.

Then came Burgoyne's caution. "You are trustees for the honour of an infant state," he argued, "and therefore Evasion, Subterfuge and Law-craft, were any man hardy enough to offer such to your Tribunal, would be to no avail." It was possible, of course, that defense testimony might "be warped unintentionally by personal favour, or the prejudice of civil contest." But honorable judges would pay no attention to bias, for "a moment's reflection upon the reputation of his country would retrieve his reason; and what his prejudice would incline him to adopt, his policy prompt him to reject."[31] The implications were obvious: Faced with possible exposure of impropriety, Americans might be shamed into behaving like proper Englishmen.

Burgoyne submitted a long list of witnesses for the prosecution. All of them were English soldiers, identified by rank and regiment. The evidence they gave was remarkably similar, as if they had rehearsed their testimony. Burgoyne insisted that he had not coached the witnesses, but since they were giving sworn statements before a commanding general, they probably understood what was expected of them. Day after day, they answered questions about Henley's behavior on Prospect Hill.

* * *

As the case against Henley unfolded, the basic narrative of events was repeated, challenged, and denied. To appreciate better the contesting legal strategies at play, we must review—sometimes point by point—the details of what may have happened on Prospect Hill. The stabbing of Corporal Reeves was, of course, a key event for the prosecution. Several witnesses—Corporal John Buchanan and Alexander Thompson in particular—recounted their sense of the events that occurred at a British barrack on December 19. According to Buchanan, the American colonel lost his temper when he heard Reeves's excuses for breaking the rules of the camp.

Buchanan recounted what happened next: "Colonel Henley reply'd, Sir, had you served me so, I would have run you thro' the body, and I believe you to be a great rascal." Reeves refused to tolerate such an insult. Buchanan remembered Reeves insisting, "I am no rascal, but a good soldier, and My officers know it." Henley wanted to halt what was becoming a slagging match. He demanded complete silence. But Reeves kept talking: "[Corporal Reeves said] I hope to be under the command of Gen. Howe, to carry arms, and fight for my king and country. Colonel Henley then said, damn your King and your country—when you had arms, you were willing to lay them down. Corporal Reeves said he was not willing to lay them down."[32]

The British witness claimed that at this moment Henley lost self-control, ordering an American guard who stood nearby "to run the rascal through." After the guard refused to obey, Henley dismounted from his horse, "seized a firelock, with a fixed bayonet," and stabbed Reeves. He was about to make another thrust when Buchanan knocked the gun away, all the while begging Henley not to kill Reeves. The colonel quickly calmed down and demanded that an American soldier place Reeves in the "guard-room." Buchanan claimed that nothing more of significance occurred after that moment, except Reeves continued to protest loudly through a window.

During the court interrogation, Glover, Tudor, and Burgoyne asked questions. The judge advocate focused on how Reeves might have provoked Henley. "Was there not something insulting in Reeves's air and manner towards Colonel Henley?" he asked. Buchanan was evasive. He did insist, however, that it was only later during a private conversation that Reeves said, "Damn the Congress and King Hancock"—a reference to the revolutionary leader John Hancock.[33]

Burgoyne and Tudor argued about the nature of the wound, which a British surgeon under oath described as "not dangerous, and did not require immediate dressing."[34] Burgoyne claimed that it was only a matter of luck that Reeves had not died. One inch toward the heart and the stab would have been fatal. Other prisoners added little to the narrative. Glover appeared most concerned about the failure of other British prisoners there to obey the American colonel's demand for silence. And then Henley himself asked a British witness, "Did I not appear to be in a good humor?" To which Robert Steel, a British sergeant, answered, "You appeared good humoured enough."[35]

Although the stabbing of an unarmed prisoner appeared from British testimony a serious breach of military responsibility, Burgoyne gave most attention as prosecutor to the events of January 8, when a confrontation between a company of American guards and a crowd of British prisoners in front of the Prospect Hill barracks resulted in three additional stabbings, none of them fatal. The challenge for Burgoyne was not simply showing that a confrontation had led to violence, but also whether Henley was culpable of anything more serious than protecting his soldiers from being mobbed by a large group of restless British prisoners. The second incident involved several hundred men, and since none of them could testify to what had occurred in other locations over a large ground, the narrative quickly fragmented into partial accounts.

Burgoyne's witnesses recounted how a company of over one hundred American guards marched from Winter Hill to Prospect Hill just before noon. When they came to a small clearing fronting one of the barracks, they encountered a sizeable number British prisoners.

The exact count was never established. Henley, who led the company, ordered the British to disperse. Since so many men were crowded into the area, the Americans and British soon got in each other's way. Suspicious that the prisoners had organized a plan to obstruct the movement of the American guards, Henley demanded that the British move off more swiftly. When they did not, he allegedly stabbed one of the slowest men with his sword. According to Arthur Leslie of the Royal Artillery, "The British soldiers turned about, and went off as fast as they could, as they were much crowded, and the road very dirty. Colonel Henley turned about, and went a little way to the right of his party, turned about again, and addressing the British soldiers, said, Damn you, I'll make you make more haste, and came up to Corporal Hadley and pushed his sword into his left side."[36]

Henley and the judge advocate pressed the witness for greater detail. Did the British soldiers "crowd the party?" Threaten them? Leslie thought not. Moreover, when interrogated by Henley, he insisted that he had not heard an order to disperse. Nor did he know anything about a specific British soldier who may have escaped American detention and was the object of an intense search. There were a lot of questions about the actual number of British prisoners. Was the group so large as to present a threat to the safety of the American guards? And could the British exiting the ground have heard Henley's orders over the noise and confusion? Did British insults provoke the Americans?

Another confrontation on January 8 merited close attention. As the American guards entered the area in front of the barracks, they jostled with the prisoners. Insults were exchanged. Thomas Page of the Twenty-Fourth Regiment explained to the court how a misunderstanding triggered violence: "I happen'd to tread on the toe of one of my comrades, and he expressed, God damn my soul; a Sergeant of the Continental guard . . . turned about, and stepped back two Or three paces, and stabbed him in the right breast, then drew the bayonet out from the man's breast, and said, Damn you, you rascal, do you damn me?"[37] The British prisoner Thomas Trudget tried to explain, but the infuriated American "pricked him a second time."[38] The guard then clubbed the British soldier in the temple with his firelock. Doctor Walker, a surgeon with the Forty-Seventh Regiment, attended the man and reported the wounds "did not appear to me to be dangerous."[39] In a separate incident, Henley stabbed a British soldier who disobeyed specific orders to return to the barracks.

However regrettable these assaults were, Burgoyne was unable to demonstrate persuasively that Henley was personally responsible for most of the assaults. The British witnesses noted that the American colonel was in another part of the field when two encounters occurred. When the judge advocate asked Thomas Page specifically about whether he saw Henley "at or near the party during the [Trudget] transaction," he responded, "I did not."[40] Another witness, Corporal William Keedley of the Ninth Regiment, informed the court about the details of the second stabbing, and when asked about Henley's exact location when it happened, he observed the American stood "in the rear of the guard-house, about thirty yards distance." Even so, the judge advocate inquired whether Henley could have diffused the situation before it turned violent. Keedley presumed that Henley "was near enough to have given any orders he pleased, but I did not hear him speak."[41] For Burgoyne, that evasive answer left open the possibility Henley had so poisoned the minds of the American guards that they attacked British soldiers without being directly ordered to do so.

* * *

On the morning of January 28, Burgoyne summed up the case for the prosecution. He delivered an impassioned speech lasting several hours. His hyperbolic rhetoric alone would have assured that everyone in the court hung on his words. Whether the presentation influenced the jurors is impossible to know, but it was certainly dramatic and immensely provocative. He expressed confidence that the parade of British witnesses had provided "such a mass of proof, as cannot be overthrown and will authorize, and call for the strongest terms I can use, in my demand for public justice." Moreover, he insisted he had scrupulously avoided unfair practices, such as trying to influence the soldiers' testimony.[42] It is important to follow his argument closely, since it framed the judge advocate's equally dramatic rebuttal.

Burgoyne spun an emotional story. He occasionally drew upon the law, but for the most part, he relied on sentiment—on accumulated feelings of injustice. He described how a defeated army, desperate to return home, had found itself at the mercies of a suspicious, often hostile host. Imagine, he asked the court, how these anxious British prisoners felt when they found themselves trapped in Cambridge. They assumed they were "entitled to a personal protection, by the general and most sacred laws of custom and reason." But no, the Americans denied them civilized treatment. How could one explain the situation? Did they not remember "we once were Brothers"?[43]

In fact, memories of the former colonial regime had not created an atmosphere of mutual understanding. The Americans regarded the British as enemies deserving no special treatment. The results were scandalous. Burgoyne reported that "men were taken up, imprisoned, and otherwise punished by the American troops." Such unacceptable practices could have been stopped, but the guards failed to do so: "It then became the indispensable duty of General Heath, to take the distribution into his own hands." His inaction allowed Henley to assert his "independency, scurrility and impiety." The stabbing of Corporal Reeves revealed the American's venomous state of mind. Instead of accepting Reeves's apology for insulting a Continental officer, Henley replied, "'Had it been me you served so, I would have run you through the body, you Rascal.'"[44] How could a proper gentleman behave in such a manner? Or excuse a second possible bayonet thrust?

Burgoyne then tried a different strategy—flattery. Would the leading officers of the Continental Army—the heroes of the Revolution—have condoned Henley's behavior? Of course, they would not. They were professional soldiers. "When I consider the actions of a Washington," Burgoyne declared, "when I meet in the field, a Gates, an Arnold,—a General Glover, and see them bravely facing death in support of the principles . . . I cannot withhold from the enemy the respect due to the soldier."[45] Burgoyne's fulsome praise may have struck the Americans as contrived, especially since Glover was the president of the court-martial. Moreover, he failed to mention Heath and the other officers Burgoyne had accused of conspiring against the British troops.[46]

Burgoyne described the disturbing events of January 8 as a "black day." Everywhere on the field before the Prospect Hill barracks Americans assaulted the defenseless prisoners. Visualize the chaotic scene, the prosecutor urged: "In one place, a party on the march are stabbing and knocking out the brains of inoffensive spectators—at another, men, under the pretense of a prisoner's escape, are glutting the same bloody purposes upon men, not pretended to be concerned—in a third, Colonel Henley in person . . . is running men through the body with his sword."[47] Burgoyne's point was not simply that Henley had resorted to unwarranted violence, but that his actions over time—his influence over the American guards—were sufficient proof of guilt. According to the law "respecting accessories and accomplices," a person encouraging someone else to engage in criminal behavior—even if he is "an hundred miles distant" at the time—shares responsibility for the crime.[48]

Burgoyne also insisted that it should make no difference to the court whether the wounds suffered by the British soldiers were superficial. He demanded to know if a person "may thrust a weapon into another's breast with impunity, provided he does not touch a mortal part." That measure was a ridiculous distinction. Responsibility for determining the severity of a stabbing would mean that the Americans "ought to establish Schools of Anatomy for the Education of young officers."[49] What mattered in such cases was the offender's intentions—his state of mind—not the death or recovery of the victim.

In addition, Burgoyne argued that it was risible to claim that the guards defended themselves out of fear of being mobbed by unarmed British prisoners. Of course, the number of British prisoners may have been as large as that of the guards. The Americans were too well trained to raise such an excuse. And they were armed. In Burgoyne's estimation, the rage witnessed on January 8 could only be explained by a "more prevalent malignity than ever appeared before in the human heart, or that the whole proceeded from the direction, order, and systematical plan."[50]

In closing, Burgoyne assured the court that a general slaughter of British prisoners had been narrowly avoided. The whole situation certainly would have spun out of control on Prospect Hill had not the British soldiers shown amazing "patience and discipline." But what of the Americans? By failing to repudiate Henley's "heinously criminal" acts, they would compromise their claim to be an honorable nation. His alleged guilt was only part of the story. The jury had to answer to future generations, to history. If a panel of Continental officers erred at this moment, they would leave a "foul and indelible blot in the first page of her [America's] new history." Like original sin, a transgression in Cambridge could never be removed by "any series of disavowal and penitence, nor ages of rectitude in government, purity in manners, inflexible faith, or the whole catalogue of public virtues." The Americans had to accept the responsibilities of independence, redeem themselves "in the opinion of mankind." The choice was clear. The jury would either restore the honor of Henley, or the honor of the country. Burgoyne insisted that the correct decision—if there was the slightest doubt—would be preservation of "the general rights of mankind."[51]

No one laughed at that moment. After a short adjournment, the court turned to the judge advocate, who presented the case for Henley. Burgoyne reserved the right to challenge Tudor's evidence. The courtroom theatrics suddenly took a surprising turn.

• CHAPTER 8 •

For the Defense

The court's attention now focused on William Tudor. He had every reason to be anxious. Only a few years out of college, he had to rebut Burgoyne, a curiously captivating figure even for many Americans. Tudor not only had to vindicate his friend David Henley's reputation but also demonstrate at a perilous moment during the war that the new nation could mount a fair trial.

Tudor rose to the challenge. In fact, throughout the ordeal, he demonstrated remarkable poise and thorough knowledge of the law. More to the point, he advanced a brilliant case effectively countering Burgoyne's theatrical speeches. The young lawyer argued persuasively that his country need not worry about its reputation in the court of world opinion. The issue was Burgoyne and the aristocratic regime he represented. The American Revolution was not on trial. What required defense was an arrogant British culture that had driven colonial Americans to declare independence.

The judge advocate opened in a straightforward manner. His pragmatic tone immediately revealed a telling contrast with how Burgoyne had conducted the prosecution. He had no interest in outlining the defense strategy in advance—certainly no desire to justify his principles. The witnesses on Henley's side would be examined, he explained, and only after the evidence had been presented would he "endeavor to lay before the Court the true state of the facts."[1]

* * *

The first group of defense witnesses addressed the stabbing of Corporal Reeves. The charge of engaging in excessive violence against a prisoner of war was difficult to counter. After all, as prosecutor, Burgoyne had presented strong testimony against Henley, leaving the impression that the attack on an innocent, unarmed man could only have resulted from the American's bloodthirsty character.

Major Swasey led the American witnesses. He gave a full account—so full that the court may have understandably wondered whether he best served the interests of the defense. He explained in detail what he remembered about the confrontation with Reeves, and his observations reinforced a lot of prosecution evidence. Swasey stated under oath that even before Henley became involved, Swasey had demanded Reeves tell him what he had done to be confined to the guardhouse. Reeves responded with a "very abusive expression." Swasey demanded silence and "threatened if he did not stop his impertinence, I would lay him over the head with my whip." Reeves refused to keep quiet. The man's failure to obey orders annoyed Henley so much that he dismounted, seized a weapon from an American guard, and "pricked" the prisoner—a remarkably gentle word for a stabbing. The argument escalated. Henley told Reeves if he said another word, "he would run him through." When Reeves "continued his insolent language, Col. Henley step'd back and made a motion to cock the firelock, and told him if he was not silent, he would blow his brains out."[2] Other British prisoners, fearful that the colonel might kill Reeves on the spot, intervened, persuading the guards to take Reeves to the guardhouse, where he would be safe. These allegations did little to counter attacks on Henley's character.

The judge advocate accommodated to the apparent damage. He certainly did not deny this basic narrative. For the defense, what mattered was not the stabbing itself, but Henley's state of mind. The question was, At the moment he seized the firelock was he intent on restoring order to the camp or attacking a drunk who protested his loyalty to the British cause? According to Swasey, Henley only wanted to silence Reeves. The major noted that Henley could have easily killed Reeves but chose not to do so. And for good reason. Reeves said nothing about America that could have provoked Henley. As Swasey explained, at no time during confrontation did Reeves "throw out any reflections upon America, or the persons concerned in the cause of it." In fact, Henley admitted that while he "damn'd Gen. Howe or his king and country," he did not blame Reeves for fighting for Great Britain. This testimony suggested that Henley was not a vicious person eager to harm unarmed prisoners—at least, not at that moment—but only a trained officer trying to control a tense situation threatening to get out of control.

Several members of the local militia, including Captain Silas Wild, confirmed Swasey's statement. They indicated the entire dispute with Reeves had turned on the demand for order and not on innate American hostility to ordinary British soldiers. Tudor asked Wild, "Do you suppose Col. Henley in the pass [with the bayonet] he made at Reeves intended to wound or only silence him?" Wild had no doubt. Henley wanted "only to silence him," and as he was giving commands, the American had spoken "very mildly." Burgoyne was skeptical, asking Wild, "Is it usual in the American service to silence men by sword and bayonet?" The militiaman responded, "No, it is not; but when the temper is raised a man will do that which at another time he would not."[3]

An honest answer, to be sure, but not a particularly helpful one for the defense. Nevertheless, Wild believed that if Henley had wanted to kill Reeves he could have done so. Elijah Horton, another witness, added, "Col. Henley might easily have wounded or killed [Reeves], had he been disposed so to do; the Colonel push'd moderately. Reeves drew back his body. The push was not sufficient to have forced the bayonet through a thick woolen cloth."[4]

After a short adjournment, the judge advocate turned to the events of January 8. The complex claims and counterclaims of that day had figured centrally in Burgoyne's case. Tudor's first witness—John Kittle, a sergeant in the militia—had no doubt what had happened on Prospect Hill. Numbers mattered. There had been more British in the clearing in front of a barrack than American guards. Although unarmed, they posed a threat to the American detachment. According to Kittle: "When we were going up Prospect-hill, the British soldiers crowded much upon us; the sergeants were obliged to fall into the ranks and exert themselves to keep the British soldiers off, they would not tho' repeatedly ordered, move out of the way." When asked about harassment, Kittle informed the court, "We were insulted by their crowding on us, laughing and sneering at the guard." He added the British deserved to be stabbed, but then, that "was my own opinion entirely."[5] Several militiamen complained of insults. One remembered a British soldier muttering, "damn the yankies," an affront that apparently triggered a serious assault on the prisoner.[6] The situation became increasingly chaotic. About five hundred British were laughing and hooting at the guard.

Only slowly did the court learn why the American guards had marched up to Prospect Hill. They had been instructed to take into custody a troublesome British soldier who, among other offenses, had forged a pass to leave the camp. Henley apparently anticipated that the prisoners might attempt to help the man escape. According to Asa Pierce, another militiaman, the colonel ordered the Americans to be on alert should the British try "to rescue him." That is exactly what happened. In the confusion before the barracks, the culprit melted into the milling prisoners, and his comrades provided cover. The crowd "laugh'd and huzza'd a good deal."[7] During the commotion Pierce pricked an agitator.

Only at that moment in the interrogation of American witnesses did it transpire that on the previous day a British prisoner had brutally attacked a sentry. The report helped explain why the guards who marched up from Winter Hill were on edge. Burgoyne reluctantly admitted for the record that "on the evening of the 7th of January, a provincial sentry was knock'd down on his post by a British soldier; that he was much beat and his gun taken from him."[8] This information meant that the militiamen involved in several stabbings were not only trying to secure a specific prisoner but also searching for the missing gun. Colonel Gerrish informed the court that about two hundred Americans under his command had surrounded a barrack where they believed the British had hidden the weapon. It was getting dark. Gerrish testified:

> A British soldier came out and said to me, damn you what do you come here for, we have done you no hurt in these barracks: We have got arms and we will shoot you. I then thought the Sentry's gun might be in that barrack, and called for a serjeant and a dozen men; they came up, then the British soldiers came to the door of the barrack and presented a weapon (I thought it had been a musket, tho' I afterwards found it had only been a club).

Gerrish contemplated opening fire but did not give the order when he realized that British soldiers in the building who had not been involved in stealing the weapon might be killed. The Americans could not find the gun, although one guard said the British had "a number of hickory sticks, shorter and stouter than walking sticks." A rumor circulated among the Americans that "there were two of our men killed."[9]

Throughout the whole fracas Henley did his best to restore order. His patience was limited, however, and when the milling group of British prisoners refused to clear the ground near the barracks quickly, Henley made a thrust with his sword "at a British soldier who was walking very slowly in front of the guard." Henry Hamson, a sergeant in the militia, provided the fullest testimony of the incident:

> As Col. Henley was walking up and down the parade, the British troops came up thick in the front of us, Col. Henley ordered them to disperse and go to their barracks, they made no movement at this order; Col Henley then moved to the left 80 or a 100 paces and looking around, found they had not moved, came back again and ordered them to go off; on this they turned and began moving very slowly, Col. Henley pushed his sword at them, but whether he wounded Any one I can't say, one of the British soldiers turned to the left And came down in the rear of me and said, damn your eyes You buggers, you shall pay for this one of these days.

Hamson could not remember whether the prisoners had insulted Henley before he "made a pass at the men," but he assured the court the British "look'd sulky and malicious."[10]

By the second week in February, Henley's ordeal was clearly winding down. No more witnesses remained. The central figures in the long trial showed signs of fatigue. It was at that moment that Tudor introduced into the court record a significant piece of evidence. He apparently did not feel compelled to comment. On December 23—in other words, well before the January 8 incident that figured so centrally in Burgoyne's case—Henley as commanding officer of the prison camp issued an order setting forth the behavior expected of all the American guards. Two sections of the document spoke directly to the allegations made against Henley. A second one stipulated, "The guards are to be vigilant and alert, and do their utmost to prevent disorders, and keep peace, ever attentive to the security of the camp." Another relevant section advised, "No offense [is] to be given to any officer or soldier of General Burgoyne's army." These words did not reveal a murderous character. Of course, one might have noted that the order appeared at the main guardhouse several days after the Reeves stabbing and might have provided cover for an earlier incident that got out of hand. However, although the document invited interpretation, Burgoyne did not comment.[11]

On January 11, the court adjourned for several days, noting, "General Burgoyne being unwell and Col. Henley asking for a few days to look over the evidence."[12] A heavy snow covered the roads. When everyone returned, Burgoyne offered a few minor observations on the American evidence. He insisted that the large hickory sticks that Gerrish had found in the British barracks were not weapons but, rather, "clubs designed to play bat and ball."[13] At that moment it was unlikely that anyone present sensed that the court-martial was about to take a sudden dramatic turn transforming the character of the entire proceedings.

* * *

On January 23, the court called upon Henley "to close his defense." He read a prepared statement stoutly maintaining his innocence. Henley did not review the specific evidence. A proper summary, he thought, was the judge advocate's responsibility. And then, in a closing reflection on his ordeal, Henley expressed confidence he would be cleared "from all the injurious and illiberal charges of Gen. Burgoyne, and that they will vindicate me for that humanity, characteristic of an American soldier, and with which the officers and soldiers of Gen. Burgoyne's late army have been treated, while I was honour'd with the command of the guards."[14]

These words may not sound particularly provocative. Nevertheless, Burgoyne took them as a personal insult. An ordinary American officer—a revolutionary no less—accused a British general, an aristocrat, and member of the House of Commons of "illiberal" behavior. Burgoyne was incensed by the audacity of the claim. He still projected arrogance, but now, his dramatic presentations contained an element of doubt, even self-pity. After all, it was he—not a colonel in the Continental Army—who championed the concept of honor against a person who had behaved "heinously criminal as an officer, and unbecoming a man; of the most indecent, violent, vindictive severity against unarmed men; and of intentional murder."[15]

Henley challenged Burgoyne, turning a court-martial into a personal affair.

* * *

Burgoyne opened his summary on a note of surprise. Henley, he claimed, had introduced an entirely new and unwelcome element to the trial. Stung by the accusation of being illiberal, he lashed out, observing that Henley had chosen "to substitute invective for argument, and to recriminate, where it was impossible to defend." Henley crossed the line defining professional conduct. During the American's statement before the court, he had the audacity to use terms "to which my ears have not been accustomed."[16] Still, Burgoyne was a proper gentleman, and, however objectionable Henley's aspersions may have been, Burgoyne insisted that he would continue to take the high moral ground. He pledged to "disavow all personal resentment." He failed. He wondered whether the court could let stand Henley's remark that Burgoyne had "done palpable dishonor to the country."[17] Would it do palpable dishonor to a country to insist that it deliver justice? he demanded. He even predicted that the court itself would be blamed if it did not condemn Henley's behavior, which, after all, only revealed an American official could not control his temper.

Still touchy about his liberal credentials, Burgoyne resumed his prosecutorial role. There was no question in his mind that the evidence he had presented "do[es] not only remain unimpeached, but [is] augmented and enforced, in the most material parts, by the evidence in defense."[18] He urged the court to consider the testimony of Major Swasey. That soldier was just as violent as Henley. Could one believe an officer who had threatened to whip Corporal Reeves? The defense could not mask the fact that Henley intended to wound, or kill, an innocent soldier. The American witnesses suspiciously forgot the details of a brazen attack. So too did Captain Wild, who confirmed Swasey's testimony, which at best had been mistaken, if not disingenuous.

Even if the American witnesses had not perjured themselves, the value of their testimony was in doubt. As Burgoyne argued, the guards were young men who seemed to have dutifully memorized their testimony. What else could one expect from "lads of sixteen years of age"? Could the words of mere boys be trusted? Apparently, mature British soldiers were not so easily influenced. As a snarky Burgoyne observed: "It was the exact tone and repetition of a fable at school, and so well was the lesson got by heart, that there was not a single difference in the arrangement of the circumstances, and scarcely a syllable misplaced. But it is not only in the similitude of memory these youths are extraordinary, they are equally remarkable in the precision of their forgetfulness."[19] It is difficult to know how a jury of American officers reacted to an attempt not only to assail the judge advocate's strategy but also to vilify young militiamen pressed into service. Many guards were, in fact, teenagers. They served at Prospect Hill because older men were fighting with George Washington. Moreover, they came from families who remembered what had happened at Lexington and Concord and, later, at Bunker Hill. A good guess is that Glover and the other members of the military panel found this line of attack objectionable.

The risk of injuring American feelings did not restrain Burgoyne. In reviewing American evidence relevant to the January 8 stabbings, he disparaged the testimony of Esell Pierce, "a lad of sixteen," who pricked a British prisoner standing in front of the barracks. Burgoyne insisted that the mind of the young man had been so indoctrinated with hatred for the British that he actually took a measure of satisfaction in running a soldier through with his bayonet. He lectured the court: "This is but one of several instances that might be selected from these proceedings, to show the degree of rancour to which the minds of the American soldiers were excited. Children that had scarcely lost the taste of their mother's Milk, grew athirst for blood: among those from whom they took the example, the Colonel thinks a man deserves death if he looks sulky, the Serjeant thinks the same if he smiles."[20]

The possibility of a general conspiracy—really a mass brainwashing practiced among revolutionary troops—raised for Burgoyne a serious legal problem. What conditions had to be satisfied for a person to be ruled an accessory to the crime committed by someone else, even by a person physically distant from the original instigator? Citing the reports of Sir Robert Foster, lord chief justice of England (1589–1663), he insisted British judges regularly dealt with such questions and accepted arguments for guilt by association. Not in America apparently; not by Tudor. Burgoyne claimed that the judge advocate refused to consider how this established principle should rightly be applied to Henley. If he had done so, he would have revealed "the enormities committed under the orders, influence, encouragement, and example of Colonel Henley when he was not present."[21]

The entire case ultimately would be decided on whether Henley and his guards experienced sufficient provocation to warrant violence against prisoners. Burgoyne admitted that there were, in fact, several incidents in which the British had misbehaved. No one could excuse knocking down a sentry. These were minor events. Nothing that had happened on Prospect Hill justified violence under the "undeniable authority of law."[22]

That claim begged the question, Whose law? Were Americans who had recently declared their independence from Great Britain obliged to accept English precedent? Burgoyne had no doubt. Separation from the mother country made no difference. His train of logic may have been correct, but in this situation, he seemed abrasively condescending. The Americans were not as free from the previous colonial regime as they liked to imagine. As Burgoyne noted, nothing had changed in legal practice: "I assume it to be undeniable, because I understand, gentlemen, that the criminal and common law of England, as well as great part of the statute law, are, not withstanding your present separation, in force and practice in your government, and that your articles of war also are almost transcript from ours."[23] It followed from this denial of cultural independence that the American jury could only deliver authentic justice if it applied the laws of England. It is not surprising that the Boston publisher of the trial record omitted Burgoyne's speech.

During his final remarks as prosecutor, the British general described himself as a martyr. He knew that Americans hated him. He had fought for principles that they did not fully understand. Their hostility made not the slightest difference. Wrapping himself in self-righteous rhetoric, Burgoyne confessed, "I know I stand in this circle at best an unpopular, with the sanguine enemies of Britain perhaps, an obnoxious character." Waxing lyrical, he reminded the court, "Implacable hatred is a scarce weed in every soil, and soon is overcome and lost under the fairer and more abundant growth of civilized humanity." Would his quixotic quest matter? His aggressive treatment of Henley might result in his own punishment. He could live with that possibility, since he believed that "I have done what I ought; that I have performed to the best of my power, my duty to my country, to the British troops under my charge, and to myself."[24]

On February 24, it was Tudor's turn. The young lawyer, fresh from training at John Adams's law offices, quickly demonstrated that he could hold his own against Burgoyne.

* * *

The judge advocate opened his summation with an apology. The trial had gone on much too long. In fact, it had become "tedious." What, he asked the court, could explain such an investment in time? The answer was General Burgoyne. His celebrity allowed him to control the pace of the proceedings. As Tudor explained, the case took on special significance not because of Henley's alleged crime, but because people were fascinated by watching a prosecutor of "distinguished rank." Every facet of Burgoyne's performance detracted from focus on the original claim that the American colonel "was appointed commandant of the garrison at Cambridge, for the purpose of executing the bloody designs of an irritated, vindictive, and sanguinary people."[25]

The normal course of justice had been influenced by more than Burgoyne's renown. For those who witnessed his theatrics, Tudor believed the general's manner of speaking posed a real challenge. The problem was not the content of his statements; it was his style. Burgoyne's turn of phrases, his way of talking, and his assumed superiority had the capacity to beguile former colonists who remembered the former imperial regime. Tudor reminded the jury that the charges against Henley had been "heightened with all the pomp of words which attic diction and tragic eloquence could furnish." Without doubt, Burgoyne was a "very able prosecutor," but he was also an actor skilled in painting in "vivid, animated colours" a range of "keen feelings and lively apprehensions."[26]

In this setting language itself was a measure of cultural difference. Tudor warned the Americans: "However excusable it may be in Gen. Burgoyne to take a partial survey of the cause; by well turn'd periods to catch the attention and force the admiration of listening crowds; and by a brilliancy of expression or affected nobility of sentiment to dazzle, the more effectually to mislead the Court, the Judge-Advocate has a very different part to act."[27]

Tudor insisted he had no need for theatrics. After all, the jury could see that the only thing missing in the general's dramatic speeches was attention to the truth. No one could say for certain why Burgoyne chose to speak in court as if he were still on the London stage. It was anyone's guess why he saw the court-martial as a means of "gaining popularity." Perhaps he just wanted to win the affection of his defeated army or promote "great political motives." Whatever the reason, Tudor insisted that as the judge advocate, he would concentrate solely on the evidence. The claim was a little disingenuous, of course, since, like any experienced trial lawyer, he knew that dramatic performance contributed to winning. Nevertheless, the call for plain speech had special appeal at the moment. He insisted, "It is my duty to exhibit facts as they arise from the evidence, stripped of the meretricious coverings which ingenuity and rhetoric have attempted to conceal."[28] The point was clear. Americans should view Burgoyne's histrionics as an index of cultural difference—a step in discovering what it meant no longer to be British.

Tudor was good to his word. He carefully reviewed the testimony. But he did a whole lot more. During his summation—lasting two days—he managed to recast the trial from a defense of Henley to a clever interrogation of British motives and behavior. The alleged mistreatment of Reeves provided an opening. Burgoyne had described the corporal's insistence on December 18 that he was not a rascal but a good soldier as a courageous act. Although the American officer seemed skeptical at the time, Reeves had remained "firm"—certainly not "insolent."[29]

Tudor asked the court what these words meant. Could firmness or insolence excuse refusal to obey an order from the commanding officer? Surely, the terms were subject to interpretation. "It has been said," the judge advocate observed, "that Reeves's behaviour was only firm, not insolent British firmness [which] often so nearly approaches insolence, that Europeans as well as Americans have been very apt to confound them." Tudor reminded the jury that he had attempted several times during the trial to get British witnesses to explain "their idea of insolence." They failed to do so, claiming under oath that it was "impossible a Briton could look insolent." What seemed insolent was really "only looking up."[30]

Tudor could not resist pointing out the political implication of this claim. "This erect countenance which they boast of," he said, "leads them to looking down upon the rest of the world, though not always with impunity." Had the court not witnessed expressions of insulting arrogance? The British thought they were superior to others—to Americans, for example. It was a telling point. Everyone in the audience had experienced imperial condescension. They knew the inability to accept colonists as equals had sparked a revolution: "Britain is feared because she is powerful. What a pity it is a nation cannot be just as well as gallant. Less pride had prevented the dismemberment of her empire, had saved the blood of thousands. And real magnanimity had e'er this arrested the hand of destruction from the heads of men, whose greatest fault (once the glorious fault of Britons!) is the love of freedom."[31] It was quite a leap from blaming the British for the war to Reeves's insistence that he was not a rascal, but that was exactly what Tudor insinuated. The ranting of a drunken soldier demonstrated why the Americans had to declare independence.

The judge advocate insisted that there was not sufficient evidence to support the charge of "intentional murder" against Henley. According to Tudor, the prosecutor would have had to demonstrate that Henley wanted to kill Reeves. But the prosecution had not been able to produce persuasive evidence that Henley was in fact driven by "murderous design." From the perspective of legal strategy, Tudor again outmaneuvered Burgoyne. Drawing extensively on the famed British jurists, such as Blackstone, Foster, and Coke, the American revealed a more solid knowledge of legal doctrine than the general possessed.[32] No one at the time commented on the irony of the argument. Tudor's mastery of British legal principles revealed that despite declaring political independence, the Americans still relied on British sources in cultural matters.

One major issue remained. Could Henley be considered an accessory to a crime even though he had not given a specific order for the American guards to stab British prisoners? The testimony had not demonstrated that the colonel was directly involved in the incident. "So far from Col. Henley's counselling, abetting, assisting or confronting the persons concerned in this action," Tudor stated, "it does not appear that he ever heard of it, till the witnesses related the fact upon oath before the Court." In his summation Burgoyne had ridiculed the notion that Henley had not personally provoked others to violence. The general believed that Henley had incited the guards. After all, "He was known to be no friend of the British soldiers; he had himself wounded one, and had been violent in his menaces against them all; he thus influenced his soldiers to stab and murder whom they pleased, if they belonged to the British army."[33]

Tudor urged the court to consider what being an accessory in wartime might involve. Burgoyne himself provided a possible answer. Before the surrender at Saratoga, the British had recruited Native Americans as allies, and in Tudor's opinion these warriors "disgraced" Burgoyne's campaign. There was no question that Tudor adopted racist language. Burgoyne had done so as well. The judge advocate described the Native Americans as "ferocious Bipeds" and "Savages." However biased he may have been, Tudor asked the jury of American officers, "Ought it to be said that because these *black* attendants knew that Gen. Burgoyne did not love Americans, that therefore he would be pleased at the butchery of the nerveless [weak] old man, defenseless female, and infant prattler?"[34] This was quite a statement coming from a man who denied the need for theatrics in court.

Tudor drew specific attention to the murder of Jane McCrea, a young woman killed by Native Americans during Burgoyne's recent campaign. The incident became the focus of American outrage. The nation's newspapers provided lurid accounts of the crime, and although Burgoyne had not ordered the attack, revolutionaries blamed him. Merely dropping McCrea's name during the trial served Tudor's purpose. After all, "if a superior in command is to be responsible for every action committed by his inferiors," the judge advocate observed, "as well might we make the General party to the murder of Miss Mackree [McCrea]?"[35]

Tudor admitted that several stabbings had occurred on January 8. But while Burgoyne held Henley personally responsible, the judge advocate reminded the court of the chaotic situation in front of the British barracks. The guards had been in pursuit of a soldier who had blatantly broken the rule of the camp. In cases of this sort British jurists are clear. They even justified homicide when it occurred as a result of official state duties. He offered the examples "where a Sheriff attempting to make a lawful arrest in a civil action or to retake one who has been arrested and made his escape, is resisted by the party and unavoidably kills him in the affray." It was a stretch to compare Henley to a sheriff in a civil matter, but the point was that a British prisoner had escaped with the help of his colleagues. These men were "too well acquainted with discipline and military severity not to know they were acting egregiously."[36]

One extremely troublesome issue remained. Henley may not have been an accessory during several stabbings, but no one could deny that he had stabbed one British soldier named Hadley who had been slow to clear the field in advance of the American guard. Tudor reconstructed the chaotic scene. The prisoners had obstructed the Americans' ability to maneuver safely; they had taunted the guard. Henley had to make a quick decision to gain control. As commander of camp, he sensed that "it had at length become absolutely necessary to convince these Britons, that there was energy enough in their guards to force obedience and curb licentiousness." Everyone was on edge, and a seasoned officer such as Henley knew the crowd of British soldiers could easily "disarm the [American] detachment by a sudden movement."[37]

The threat had been real. But the perception of danger aside, the British had not in fact been armed. And so, the question remained, Could Henley's wounding of an uncooperative soldier be excused as the justified reaction to chaotic disorder or did his actions result from "impetuosity"? The jury faced a hard decision.

> If Gentlemen you should be satisfied, that Hadley at the time he was wounded, was moving off, you will consider whether Col. Henley is not very blame-worthy for making a violent lunge into a man's body, who was obeying his orders and getting out of the way—should you be convinced that Hadley was not removing, though such preemptory and repeated orders were given him with his comrades to retire to their barracks, your opinion will be different.[38]

The judge advocate had no need to remind the jurors that the entire trial was without precedent. Within this strange context, Americans and British took the measure of each other. Burgoyne had demanded special privileges and, as prosecutor, depicted Henley as a vicious person who, if allowed to go unpunished for his actions, would degrade the international standing of the United States. The general appealed to honor. Tudor argued that Henley had behaved in a responsible way. If one understood the context of his decisions—provocation and confusion—one would see the use of excessive force as justified.

The problem of how to draw the line between the necessary application of force and self-control in a situation of extreme stress defies easy answers. We face the same challenges today. Incidents of excessive force turn ultimately not only on the guilt or innocence of people acting in the name of authority, but on a society's willingness to seriously entertain the topic at all. Tudor and Burgoyne—Heath and Henley as well—measured the country's reputation on its ability to deliver unbiased justice. The Americans hoped they could do so; the British expressed doubts. All the judge advocate could say to the court at the end of the ordeal was, "I doubt not your judgment will vindicate the justice of our country, and be approved by the honest and impartial wherever it shall be known."[39]

* * *

Beyond the confines of the courthouse, people closely monitored the proceedings, coming to their own conclusions about Henley's guilt and Burgoyne's showy speeches. They followed the parade of witnesses. These men and women comprised a public trying to comprehend the burden of independence through the lens of a dramatic trial. For Burgoyne, of course, the public he worried about was a very small group in London. He was obsessed with the reactions of a distant king and government ministers embarrassed by the defeat at Saratoga. The public of Henley and Heath is more significant for our purposes, although difficult precisely to describe. One possibility for better understanding the thinking of this nebulous group is inviting. Contemporary newspapers and personal letters provide a window into the sentiments of people trying to make sense of the Revolution.

Weekly journals published in Boston and Worcester ran lively opinion pieces. This commentary helps us to imagine conversations in taverns and private homes. It was in such places where Americans grappled with what it meant no longer to be British. One paper published a mission statement that would serve well for our own society. The editor claimed "the diffusion of knowledge, essentially necessary in promoting the most important interests of society, is undoubtedly effected, in some measure, by the circulation of newspapers." Without them, revolutionary Americans would have been unable to learn about "the despotic measures and deep-laid plots of a British court."[40]

It is significant that the content of these papers is not what one would expect. Subscribers were not instructed about the noble principles that had allegedly energized separation from Great Britain. Perhaps they took such topics for granted. Or, what a small group of founding fathers chronicled. Nevertheless, there was almost no evidence in the discussions of 1778 of what we might call a coherent political ideology. More common were emotional themes—contempt for aristocratic privilege, disdain for arrogant behavior, ridicule of pompous language, and most surprising, insistence that whatever the British might think, Americans were as worthy of respect throughout the world as were their former rulers. Cultural independence acquired meaning in a swirl of perceived insult and insecurity.

Hannah Winthrop, who kept her friend Mercy Otis Warren informed of events in Cambridge, left a caustic account of the trial. Her marvelously informative letters left no doubt about her revolutionary credentials. However committed to independence she may have been, her comments suggest how general perceptions of character—the stuff of emotionally charged impressions—reinforced political ideas. Winthrop felt it was outrageous that American authorities had allowed Henley's court-martial to go forward. What had he done to deserve such treatment? "For doing his duty in preventing an insurrection of British troops," she concluded. Even more distressing, Burgoyne had taken it "upon himself to Preside, interrogating & aiming to intimidate Witnesses on our part, encouraging those on his own." Whether the charge was true or not did not matter in the public forum. She was convinced the British general had perverted the true course of justice. He had done so by "displaying his Parliamentary Eloquence, Spouting forth his Contempt of Americans, sometimes in insidious Ironical compliments, and others by open direct abuse." In dazzling language so insulting to the American ear, he had painted Henley "in the blackest colors." Even more objectionable, he had treated General Glover, the hero of the famed Delaware River crossing, with contempt. In Winthrop's opinion, the whole performance exhibited "the haughtiness of an Emperor."[41]

The newspaper analysis was anonymous. Writers—often the editor—submitted pieces over the name of a Roman or seventeenth-century English political figure. Of course, it would be a stretch to claim that these journal essays reflected the opinions of ordinary people, but the weekly publications certainly reached a wide readership. The press runs were normally about one thousand copies. But the newspapers reached a much greater number in taverns and coffee shops. During the court-martial, four journals circulated in eastern Massachusetts.

Rejection of an aristocratic society dominated the commentary. Contempt for class privilege comes as a surprise, since for a very long time Massachusetts had been governed by well-connected men appointed by the king. New Englanders were familiar with the rituals of monarchical rule. Times had changed—and quickly. The experience of dealing with Burgoyne reminded people how far they had come in only a few short years.

Those people who followed the trial seemed surprised to discover how much the British looked down on the Americans. A sense of superiority was conspicuous whenever ordinary soldiers as well as their officers conversed with the former colonists. British haughtiness was insufferable. "Andrew Marvell"—whose pen name was taken from the seventeenth-century poet who had worked with Oliver Cromwell and defended republican ideas—submitted his opinions to the *Boston Gazette,* observing that even "the lower class of people" were repelled by British arrogance. He claimed it was hard for Americans to extend hospitality to the prisoners on Prospect Hill because of "the insolence peculiar to British troops, who conceive themselves to be the chosen of the world." An obnoxious "idea of superiority over Americans" allows the British to "speak of them as their subjects."

In another essay, Sydney chastised local revolutionaries for trying to be polite to the British. Why bother making an effort for people who projected such a strong belief in their own self-importance? "I say superiority," Sydney ranted, "for is it not evident from the whole tenor of their conduct that they look upon themselves as superior beings, and we are their vassals?" It was the lot of poor Henley to endure "the arrogant demand of the British prisoner [who] calls a court-martial to try the worthy Colonel, not for firing upon the banditti, where he is alone capable, but for drawing a few drops of blood from villains [who] ought to have paid their lives for their insolence." Americans had to find a way to teach the British "to respect us as freemen."[42]

In the swirl of popular opinion, Burgoyne became a symbol of a corrupt aristocratic regime in which titles and sinecures reflected privilege rather than merit. The newspapers described him sarcastically as "Lieutenant-General in the service of his Britannic Majesty, Colonel of the Queen's Regiment of Dragoons, Governor of Fort William in North Britain, a Member of the British parliament, &c. &c. &c."[43] American rejection of such favoritism was most evident during a wartime debate over how captured Continental soldiers should be exchanged for British prisoners.

One commentator, identified as "Hortentius," devised an ingenious plan. Since the British regarded themselves as superior to Americans, he suggested treating each of Burgoyne's honors as if it represented a separate person, so that, for every distinction he listed, a number of Americans would be exchanged. "One prisoner [Burgoyne] therefore have twenty different offices; or such greater or less number as shall, with respect to rank," Hortentius explained. "This being admitted I think the General is the most profitable prisoner we could have taken, having more offices, or (what amounts to the same thing in Old England) more titles, than any Gentleman on this side of the Ganges." The author observed in his own listing of honors, Burgoyne always ended with a series of etceteras—as in "etc., etc." Hortentius associated these abbreviations with "cabalistic signs."[44]

In practice, the clever formula possessed its own logic. First came Burgoyne's standing as a colonel of the Queen's Regiment of light dragoons. Hortentius argued, "As the British troops naturally prize everything in proportion as it partakes in royalty, and undervalues whatever originates from a republican government, I suppose a Colonel of her Majesty's own regiment will procure at least three Continental Colonels of horse." Burgoyne valued his position as the governor of Fort William, a source of personal income requiring no particular duties. For this entry on the general's résumé, the Americans might expect two governors in return. Hortentius weighed the worth of each title, concluding that in exchange for Burgoyne the Americans could demand "two Major Generals, three Colonels of light horse, two Governors, one member of Congress, the Admiral of our own navy, one Commander in Chief in a separate department, and six Privates, which is probably more than this extraordinary hero could fetch in any part of Great Britain, were he exposed at public auction."[45]

However vain and pompous he may have been, Burgoyne posed an easily overlooked threat to a culture not yet comfortable with independence. He was a Siren-like figure enticing naïve Americans to return to a former, more sophisticated regime. During the trial, Tudor had warned that language—slang words—were a means of diminishment. Witnesses repeatedly testified to the sting of British insults. Guards were called "Yankeys" and "rebels," both viewed as highly derogatory terms. The Americans countered by labeling the prisoners as "rascals," but that was not the same. The response betrayed a defensiveness, a sense perhaps that the former colonists were not quite the equals of the British.

It was in this tense environment that a newspaper writer expressed shock "that some of my countrymen should be so far deceived by the studied eloquence of this pleading General; as to take his imprudent irony and witty sarcasms for well-placed compliments on the country." He mocked the Americans, and they often did not perceive the danger. Sydney feared that Burgoyne's "many magnificent titles [may] dazzle a young people, unacquainted with these fopperies of distinction."[46]

To compensate for their defensiveness, Americans overcompensated, urging fellow revolutionaries to demonstrate toughness. They should start by unequivocally supporting Henley's honor. The entire trial represented an embarrassment for the new nation. As one writer advised, "Let any general in command, let any officer, let any citizen look thro' the pages of history and produce an instance of an enemy subjugated, having it in their power, by arrogant demand, to put an officer of rank under arrest."[47] In another newspaper, "Adolphus" insisted that it was time for Americans to respond to British insults. Doing so "will show her that we are determined to be trampled on no longer—it will teach her to respect us as freemen . . . we have couched to insult long enough—for the future let us act with that resolution which should make the character of an independent people."[48]

"Andrew Marvell" made the strongest appeal for Americans to act as genuine Americans, to demonstrate two years after the publication of the Declaration of Independence that they were really independent and not just marginalized English people. In a long essay Marvell reminded readers that independence was more than a paper claim; it was a source of identity—a way of living:

> [We] wish to see a manly, determined spirit, such as should convince these sons of pride and war, that they are not to trample upon the rights of mankind with impunity, such as to convince them that they are but the same species, holding no higher rank in the scale of beings, than Americans. . . . At best, they are but our fellow worms . . . they have no better right to superiority over us, than a Frenchman, a Spaniard, or native of Japan. Why should a people, declaring themselves independent of their [British] Government consider themselves in any other light?[49]

* * *

The verdict probably surprised no one—not even Burgoyne. After conferring very briefly, the court cleared Henley of all charges and restored him as commander of the prison camp. Tudor had constructed an impressive defense, whereas Burgoyne too often substituted theatrics for persuasive evidence. Still, once we have reviewed the testimony of British and American soldiers, it is hard to decide whether Henley had used excessive force against unarmed prisoners. Much of the trial focused on his mood, on possible motives for behavior unbecoming an officer and gentleman. Was he simply trying to restore order, avoid a dangerous situation which could easily expose prison guards to violence? Or, as Heath suggested, did a respected American colonel fail during a stressful confrontation to control his temper? Perhaps Continental officers such as Heath and Glover were determined from the beginning to exonerate a respected soldier. Whether he acted professionally or not, Henley managed to put the American Revolution on trial, raising questions about national honor that have never been fully resolved.

After "mature consideration," the jury determined that there would never again be another trial of this sort. Too many concessions had been made; flexible procedures had allowed an imprisoned general to challenge the country's ability to deliver justice. The last entry in the shorthand trial records explains that although

Burgoyne had insisted on serving as the prosecutor, he had drawn on British practice. The court had acquiesced to his demands.

No more. His behavior was "altogether novel in the proceedings of any court martial in the army of the United States of America." In the future, the judge advocate would handle the responsibilities of the prosecutor. The court noted that Burgoyne's performance had been "both tedious and expensive" and should not be "drawn into precedent."[50] The decision amounted to a belated declaration of independence, a determination by some revolutionaries that the country was now prepared to go forward on its own.

• EPILOGUE •

After Cambridge

General Burgoyne repeatedly warned American authorities that the civilized world was closely monitoring the Henley trial. These observers allegedly wanted to know whether the United States was mature enough to deliver justice in a case involving difficult ethical issues. But, in fact, no foreign government—not even Great Britain—showed interest in the final verdict. Certainly, France was not concerned about the outcome of a bizarre court-martial. In February 1778 it recognized the independence of the United States. The Convention Army remained in America, trapped by failed negotiations, and it was not until 1783 that the last of Burgoyne's soldiers were allowed to return home.[1]

The Americans' unwillingness to convict Henley did not surprise Burgoyne. After squabbling with Congress over financial details, he departed for the final time from the United States. He was preoccupied with the political challenges awaiting him in London. Rightly so, since he never managed to restore his reputation with the king or the ministers directing the war effort. Ironically, he begged the king to grant him a court-martial so that he could defend his decisions during the Northern campaign. As happens so often in such situations, government ministers were eager not to review publicly the details of an embarrassing defeat. After failing to defend his honor, Burgoyne returned to his first love—the theater.

On April 2, Burgoyne had one last conversation with General Heath, with whom he had been bickering for many months. The British officer was determined to depart on a positive note. The two men dined—as they had soon after Burgoyne's defeated army reached Cambridge in November—and in a generous, although condescending gesture, he said, "I know your situation, Sir, and the difficulty of obtaining many foreign necessaries you may want or wish." If Heath provided a list of desired items, Burgoyne promised to ship them back to Boston once he had reached London. In his memoir published some years later, Heath took pride in resisting an appeal to the soft colonialism that had once held the British Empire together. Writing in the third person, Heath explained, "Our General thanked him for his politeness, but was careful not to mention any [items], choosing rather to suffer with his fellow countrymen the necessities of the times, than to avail himself of so exclusive a favour."[2] Heath lived long into the nineteenth century, a New England farmer once again who enjoyed telling visitors—sometimes at excessive length—about his close friendship with George Washington.[3]

Henley never overcame his resentment over an ordeal he felt was entirely undeserved. He despised Burgoyne. He regarded Burgoyne's charges as an insult not only to him but also to his country. Just as the British general was leaving Massachusetts, the two men apparently arranged a duel. It is hard to tell whether either was serious. Henley seems to have issued the challenge. The American colonel was prohibited from participating in such an event so long as he remained a Continental officer. The engagement was, therefore, scheduled to take place in Bermuda after the conclusion of the war. Not surprisingly, by 1783, when the peace treaty was signed, the two men had gone their separate ways.[4]

However much he complained about a humiliating trial, Henley had an impressive career, much of it owing to George Washington's trust. The colonel soon left his post at Prospect Hill and joined the American intelligence service operating outside British-occupied New York City. He provided Washington with regular reports on troops' movements. After the war, Henley established a business supplying the American army with cloth for uniforms. And in 1790 Washington appointed Henley as agent of the Department of War for the Southwest Territory. He moved to Knoxville, where he demanded strong law and order. He performed his responsibilities well—a street and bridge were named after him—dying in 1823 after a long career in government service.[5]

A remarkable record of a conversation that took place soon after the trial has survived. William Tudor encountered Henley on a visit to family in Roxbury. Understandably, Tudor expected Henley to show some gratitude for his inspired defense at the court-martial. But Henley would have none of it. He was clearly upset. It turned out that Henley had been courting a local woman, Sarah. He believed that she was not receptive because she had learned from the court proceedings that Henley "was a man of a passionate, Impetuous temper." He told a perplexed Tudor, "You have destroyed my happiness. You may now do me a favor to shoot me."[6] Tudor had no interest in killing Henley, and they soon restored an old friendship. And Henley did manage to persuade Sarah to marry him.

Tudor went on to become a leading Boston attorney and minor literary figure. In 1796 he traveled to England, where he met with George III. Upon hearing the American's name, he declared Tudor a distant cousin. It was reported, "The interview continued so long that the lord-in-waiting growing impatient, said 'His majesty seems so deeply engaged with his cousin that he forgets what a number of persons are waiting to be presented.'"[7] The king apparently forgot how, two decades earlier, the English who ruled an empire looked down on the likes of Tudor.

* * *

Early twentieth-century photograph of tower at Prospect Hill. (From *Haskell's Historical Guidebook of Somerville;* Collection of the Massachusetts Historical Society)

Today, a four-story castle stands atop of Prospect Hill. Like a curious structure encountered in a W. G. Sebald novel, it has a mysterious, out-of-place quality. The tower was constructed of dark granite in 1904, an imposing monument marking the spot where once Washington's troops besieging Boston after the Battle of Bunker Hill surveyed an encircled British army. The Hill later became a prisoner-of-war camp. The inspiration for the American castle is hard to understand. We wonder why the architect designed what looks like an ancient fortification—an English folly out of place. Whatever his intentions may have been, his creation is imposing, an unexpected reminder of a distant era when soft colonialism ruled an empire by a thread.

And it might remind some visitors of a moment during the Revolution when thousands of communities throughout the United States confronted what it meant not to be British in a new country. What made us different? The answers they devised made sense within the context of their own experience—a tension between tradition and change—and over time, these local stories merged into larger stories about independence, about abstract principles of honor and justice, and about how Americans hoped people in an expanding world would regard them. It sparked a revolutionary conversation—one informed by insecurity and pride—that continues to this day.

• ACKNOWLEDGMENTS •

Over the years a number of generous people have offered valuable insights into the Henley Trial. Some of them read the entire manuscript, saving me from embarrassing mistakes and suggesting fresh lines of interpretation. I thank them for their support: Patrick Griffin, Philip Zea, Walter Woodward, Joyce E. Chaplin, Stephen W. Schwab, Richard Bartecki, Michael Lammert, Charles Carter, and Sarah Breen. Christopher Sparshott provided welcome help analyzing the court records. Special thanks go to Charles M. Sullivan, Executive Director, Cambridge Historical Commission, who alerted me to eighteenth-century drawings of the building where the court-martial was held and of the prison camp on Prospect Hill. David Carlson, University of Notre Dame, supplied valuable research assistance. I also greatly appreciate the Northwestern University Library, which allowed me access to essential digital collections. And as always, Susan C. Breen provided crucial editorial guidance at every stage.

• NOTES •

1. SOFT COLONIALISM

1. Michael D. Hattem provides a full account of how Americans over more than two centuries have interpreted the meaning of the Revolution in *The Memory of '76: The Revolution in American History* (Yale University Press, 2024).
2. The experiences of ordinary Americans during the Revolution are the focus of T. H. Breen, *The Will of the People: The Revolutionary Birth of America* (Harvard University Press, 2019); Barbara Clark Smith, *The Freedoms We Lost: Consent and Resistance in Revolutionary America* (New Press, 2010); and Ray Raphael, *A People's History of the American Revolution: How Common People Shaped the Fight for Independence* (New Press, 2016).
3. See Kariann Akemi Yokota, *Unbecoming British: How Revolutionary America Became a Postcolonial Nation* (Oxford University Press, 2011); Sam W. Haynes, *Unfinished Revolution: The Early American Republic in a British World* (University of Virginia Press, 2010); Eric Nelson, *The Royalist Revolution: Monarchy and the American Founding* (Harvard University Press, 2014); Johann Neem, "American History in a Golden Age," *History and Theory* 50 (2011): 41–70; and Joyce Appleby, "Recovering America's Historic Diversity: Beyond Exceptionalism," *Journal of American History* 79 (1992): 419–31.
4. For example, Christian McBurney, *George Washington's Nemesis: The Outrageous and Unfair Court-Martial of Major General Charles Lee During the Revolutionary War* (Savas Beatie, 2020).

5. For a very different revolutionary court-martial, see McBurney, *George Washington's Nemesis.*
6. See T. H. Breen, Kathleen Duval, Leslie M. Harris, Michael D. Hattem, and Serena Zabin, "The Revolution at 250: A Conversation," *Journal of the Early Republic* 44 (2024): 513–79.
7. Jack P. Greene, *The Constitutional Origins of the American Revolution* (Cambridge University Press, 2010); Edmund S. Morgan, *The Birth of the Republic, 1763–89* (University of Chicago Press, 2012); Gordon S. Wood, *The American Revolution: A History* (Penguin Random House, 2002).
8. Yokota, *Unbecoming British.*
9. My interpretation draws on the work of Frantz Fanon, especially his *A Dying Colonialism* (Grove Atlantic, 1964). Also helpful were Ashis Nandy, *The Intimate Enemy: Loss and Recovery of Self Under Colonialism* (Oxford University Press, 1983); Lorenzo Veracini, *Settler Colonialism: A Theoretical Overview* (Springer, 2024); Akshya Saxena, *Vernacular English: Reading the Anglophone in Postcolonial India* (Princeton University Press, 2022); and Robert J. C. Young, *Postcolonialism: An Historical Introduction* (Wiley, 2016).
10. Ignacio Gallop-Diaz, Andrew Shankman, and David J. Silverman, eds., *Anglicizing America: Empire, Revolution, Republic* (University of Pennsylvania Press, 2015); John M. Murrin, "Anglicizing an American Colony: The Transformation of Provincial Massachusetts" (Ph.D. diss, Yale University, 1966); Brendan McConville, *The King's Three Faces: The Rise and Fall of Royal America, 1688–1776* (University of North Carolina Press, 2006).
11. Douglas R. Egerton, *Death or Liberty: African Americans and Revolutionary America* (Oxford University Press, 2009).
12. Linda Colley, *Britons: Forging the Nation 1707–1837* (Yale University Press, 2009); T. H. Breen, "Ideology and Nationalism on the Eve of the American Revolution: Revisions Once More in Need of Revising," *Journal of American History* 84 (1997): 13–39.
13. The best account is Fred Anderson, *Crucible of War: The Seven Years' War and the Fate of Empire in British North America* (Knopf, 2001).
14. *New-Hampshire Gazette,* 13 July 1764.
15. T. H. Breen, *The Marketplace of Revolution: How Consumer Politics Shaped American Independence* (Oxford University Press, 2004).
16. James A. Henretta, *"Salutary Neglect": Colonial Administration Under the Duke of Newcastle* (Princeton University Press, 1972).

17. Benjamin Franklin, *The Papers of Benjamin Franklin,* ed. Leonard W. Labaree, vol. 13 (2024), 127–29.
18. Jan De Vries, *The Industrious Revolution: Consumer Behavior and the Household Economy, 1650 to the Present* (Cambridge University Press, 2008); Maxine Berg, *Luxury and Pleasure in Eighteenth-Century Britain* (Oxford University Press, 2005); Breen, *Marketplace of Revolution.*
19. William Eddis, *Letters from America,* ed. Aubrey C. Land (Belknap Press of Harvard University Press, 1969), 51–52.
20. Benjamin Franklin to Lord Howe, 20 July 1776, in *Papers of Benjamin Franklin,* vol. 22 (online).
21. Benjamin Trumbull, *A Discourse, Delivered at the Anniversary Meeting of the Freemen of the Town of New-Haven, April 12, 1773* (New Haven, CT, 1773), 20–21.
22. Thomas Jefferson's "original Rough draught" of the Declaration of Independence, in *Papers of Thomas Jefferson,* vol. 1: *1760–1776,* ed. Julian Boyd (Princeton University Press, 1950), 423–27.
23. Thomas Pownall, *The Administration of the Colonies* (London, 1764), 28.
24. Abigail Adams to Catharine Sawbridge Macaulay, 1774, Founders Online, National Archives.
25. William Tudor, *An Oration Delivered March 5th, 1779* (Boston, 1779), 8, 14–15.

2. THEATER OF WAR

1. On the American reaction to Britain's military occupation, see T. H. Breen, "Empire and Resistance: Reflections on the American and Irish Revolutions," in *Ireland and America: Empire, Revolution, and Sovereignty,* ed. Patrick Griffin and Francis D. Cogliano (University of Virginia Press, 2021), 69–87.
2. See Donald F. Johnson, *Occupied America: British Military Rule and the Experience of Revolution* (University of Pennsylvania Press, 2023).
3. Cited in Bernard Donoughue, *British Politics and the American Revolution: The Path to War, 1773–1775* (Macmillan, 1964), 49.
4. Edward Barrington De Fonblanque, *Political and Military Episodes [. . .] Derived from the Life and Correspondence of the Right Hon. John Burgoyne* (London, 1876), 135.
5. Francis Josiah Hudleston, *Gentleman Johnny Burgoyne: Misadventures of an English General in the Revolution* (Bobbs-Merrill, 1927), 52.

6. Hannah Winthrop to Mercy Otis Warren, circa May 1775, Massachusetts Historical Society, Digital Collections; hereafter cited as MHS.
7. Abigail Adams to John Adams, 25 July 1775, Adams Family Papers, MHS.
8. My understanding of Burgoyne's personal life and military career before the Battle of Saratoga draws upon the splendid research of Fonblanque in his *Political and Military Episodes.* Also valuable are Andrew O'Shaughnessy, *The Men Who Lost America: British Command During the Revolutionary War and the Preservation of the Empire* (Yale University Press, 2012), 123–64; "John Burgoyne: Ambitious General," in *George Washington's Opponents: British Generals and Admirals in the American Revolution,* ed. George Athan Billias (William Morrow, 1969), 142–92; and Norman S. Poser, *From the Battlefield to the Stage: The Many Lives of General John Burgoyne* (McGill-Queen's University Press, 2022).
9. Cited in Piers Mackesy, *The War for America, 1775–1783* (Harvard University Press, 1964), 108.
10. John Burgoyne, *The Maid of the Oaks: A New Dramatic Entertainment* (London, 1774), Eighteenth-Century Collections Online.
11. John Burgoyne, *The Speech of a General Officer in the House of Commons, February 20th, 1775* (Boston, 1775), 6.
12. Cited in Hudleston, *Gentleman Johnny Burgoyne,* 51.
13. *Copy of Gen. Burgoyne's Answer to Gen. Lee's Letter* (Boston, 1775), 1.
14. *Copy of Gen. Burgoyne's Answer to Gen. Lee's Letter,* 1.
15. Cited in T. H. Breen, *American Insurgents, American Patriots: The Revolution of the People* (Macmillan, 2010), 244–47.
16. Cited in Max M. Mintz, *The Generals of Saratoga: John Burgoyne and Horatio Gates* (Yale University Press, 1990), 55.
17. "Copy of Manifesto Issued by Lieut. Genl. Burgoyne," June 24th, 1777, in Douglas R. Cubbison, *Burgoyne and the Saratoga Campaign: His Papers* (University of Oklahoma Press, 2012), 201–3.
18. Fonblanque, *Political and Military Episodes,* 117.
19. Fonblanque, *Political and Military Episodes,* 146–49.
20. Fonblanque, *Political and Military Episodes,* 153.
21. "To Lord George Germain," 20 August 1775, in *A Memorial of the American Patriots Who Fell at the Battle of Bunker Hill* (Boston, 1896), 160.
22. Cited in Richard Frothingham, *History of the Siege of Boston and the Battles of Lexington, Concord, and Bunker Hill* (Boston, 1851), 328.
23. James Thacher, *A Military Journal During the American Revolutionary War* (Kellock Roberston, 2009), 44; Abigail Adams to John Adams, 25 October 1777, MHS.

24. Justin Winsor, *The Memorial History of Boston* (Boston, 1882), vol. 2, 73; Everett W. Burdett, *History of the Old South Meeting House* (Boston, 1877), chap. 7; Benjamin B. Winsor, *The History of the Old South Church in Boston* (Boston, 1830).
25. *Memoirs of Major-General William Heath,* ed. William Abbatt (New York, 1901) (originally published in Boston, 1798); hereafter cited as Heath, *Memoirs.*
26. Cited in Saratoga National Historical Park, New York, online.
27. David Ramsay, *The History of the American Revolution,* ed. Lester H. Cohen (Liberty Fund, 1990), 624.
28. Heath, *Memoirs,* advertisement before title page, and 1.
29. Heath, *Memoirs,* 19.
30. Francis S. Drake, *The Town of Roxbury; Its Memorable Persons and Places* (Boston Municipal Printing Office, 1905), 390.
31. Heath, *Memoirs,* 13.
32. Heath, *Memoirs,* 19.
33. Cited in Drake, *Town of Roxbury,* 26.
34. See Joseph A. Comforti, *Imagining New England: Explorations of Regional Identity from the Pilgrims to the Mid-Twentieth Century* (University of North Carolina Press, 2001), 1–122.
35. Edmund S. Morgan, *The Meaning of Independence: John Adams, George Washington, and Thomas Jefferson* (University of Chicago, 1976), 3–58.
36. Heath, *Memoirs,* 1.
37. Heath, *Memoirs,* 1.
38. Amos Adams, *A Concise, Historical View* (Boston, 1769).
39. On the role of religion in revolutionary mobilization, see T. H. Breen, *The Will of the People: The Revolutionary Birth of America* (Harvard University Press, 2019), 54–85.
40. Adams, *A Concise, Historical View,* 8, 49–52.
41. Zachariah G. Whitman, *The History of the Ancient and Honorable Artillery Company* (Boston, 1842), 300–301.
42. John Lathrop, *A Sermon Preached to the Ancient and Honorable Artillery Company in Boston* (Boston, 1774), 19.
43. Lathrop, *A Sermon Preached to the Ancient and Honorable Artillery Company in Boston,* 23, 43.
44. Drake, *Town of Roxbury,* 26.
45. Heath, *Memoirs,* 1.
46. Cited in *Frederick the Great on the Art of War,* ed. Jay Luvaas (Da Capo, 1966), 77. See also Tim Blanning, *Frederick the Great: King of Prussia*

(Penguin Random House, 2016). Heath's view is detailed in *Boston Gazette*, 18 February 1771 and 27 September 1773.

47. Fred Anderson, *A People's Army: Massachusetts Soldiers and Society in the Seven Years' War* (University of North Carolina Press, 1984).
48. "A Military Countryman," *Boston Gazette*, 18 February 1771.
49. "A Military Countryman," *Boston Gazette*, 18 February 1771.
50. "A Military Countryman," *Boston Gazette*, 18 February 1771.
51. *Boston Gazette*, 26 September 1774 (emphasis in original).
52. *Boston Gazette*, 26 September 1774.
53. *Boston Gazette*, 26 September 1774.
54. John Adams to William Heath, 14 December 1807, Founders Online, National Archives.
55. John Adams to William Heath, 11 May 1807, Founders Online.
56. "A Military Countryman," *Boston Gazette*, 26 September 1774.
57. See Quentin Skinner, *Liberty as Independence: The Making and Unmaking of a Political Ideal* (Cambridge University Press, 2025), chap. 6.
58. James Warren to John Adams, 27 June 1775, MHS.
59. Cited in Hudleston, *Gentleman Johnny Burgoyne*, 72.
60. Cited in G. D. Scull, ed., *The Evelyns in America: Compiled from Family Papers and Other Sources, 1608–1805* (Oxford, 1881), 189–90.
61. Henry Hulton, *Henry Hulton and the American Revolution: An Outsider's Inside View*, ed. Neil Longley York (Colonial Society of Massachusetts, 2010), 348.
62. George Washington to John Hancock, 8 January 1775, in *Papers of George Washington* (Revolutionary War Series), vol. 2, 69; Washington to the Board of War, 29 July 1776, ibid., vol. 5, 492; Scull, *The Evelyns*, 189.
63. Mercy Otis Warren, *The Blockheads: Or, The Affrighted Officers* (Boston, 1776), 1, 4.
64. Fonblanque, *Political and Military Episodes*, 208–9.

3. ENCOUNTERS ON THE ROAD

1. *Acts and Resolves, Public and Private of the Province of the Massachusetts Bay* (1918), vol. 20, 184; *Continental Journal* (Boston), 13 November 1777; *The Literary Diary of Ezra Stiles*, ed. Franklin Bowditch Dexter (Scribner's Sons, 1901), vol. 2, 221; Justin Winsor, *The Memorial History of Boston* (Boston, 1882), vol. 3, 183.

2. Abigail Adams to John Adams, 25 October 1775, Adams Papers, Massachusetts Historical Society, Digital Collections; hereafter cited as MHS.
3. Frank Moore, *Diary of the American Revolution* (New York, 1865), vol. 1, 513.
4. William Tudor to John Adams, 27 June 1775, Adams Papers, MHS.
5. *Memoirs of Major-General William Heath,* ed. William Abbatt (New York, 1901), 251 (originally published in Boston, 1798); hereafter cited as Heath, *Memoirs.*
6. See T. Cole Jones, *Captives of Liberty: Prisoners of War and the Politics of Vengeance in the American Revolution* (University of Pennsylvania Press, 2020); and Ken Miller, *Dangerous Guests: Enemy Captives and Revolutionary Communities During the War for Independence* (Cornell University Press, 2014).
7. Heath, *Memoirs,* 252.
8. Cited in Sylvia R. Frey, *The British Soldier in America: A Social History of Military Life in the Revolutionary Period* (University of Texas Press, 1981), 139.
9. Edward Barrington De Fonblanque, *Political and Military Episodes [. . .] Derived from the Life and Correspondence of the Right Hon. John Burgoyne* (London, 1876), 316–17.
10. Cited in Fonblanque, *Political and Military Episodes,* 318.
11. See Richard Brookhiser, *Glorious Lessons: John Trumbull, Painter of the American Revolution* (Yale University Press, 2024); and Jules David Prown, *Art as Evidence: Writings on Art and Material Culture* (Yale University Press, 2001), 159–87.
12. Not surprisingly, the exact numbers vary substantially. I have followed Andrew O'Shaughnessy, *The Men Who Lost America: British Command During the Revolutionary War and the Preservation of the Empire* (Yale University Press, 2012), 146–47.
13. Roger Lamb, *Memoir of His Own Life* (Dublin, 1811), 204.
14. The British surrender at Saratoga has generated an impressive number of studies. I have relied on Fonblanque, *Political and Military Episodes,* chap. 4; O'Shaughnessy, *The Men Who Lost America,* 138–59; Max M. Mintz, *The Generals of Saratoga: John Burgoyne and Horatio Gates* (Yale University Press, 1990), chaps. 9–20; Kevin J. Weddle, *The Complete Victory: Saratoga and the American Revolution* (Oxford University Press, 2021); Douglas R. Cubbison, *Burgoyne and the Saratoga Campaign: His Papers* (University of Oklahoma Press, 2012); and Piers Mackesy,

The War for America 1775–1783 (Harvard University Press, 1964), 130–60.

15. "Copy of Manifesto Issued by Lieut. Genl. Burgoyne," in Cubbison, *Burgoyne and the Saratoga Campaign,* 201–3.
16. John Burgoyne, *State of the Expedition from Canada: As Laid Before the House of Commons* (London, 1780), 99–100.
17. Burgoyne, *State of the Expedition from Canada,* 101.
18. Cited in Fonblanque, *Political and Military Episodes,* 306.
19. "Copy of Second Message from Lieut. Genl. Burgoyne to Major General Gates," 20 October 1777, in Cubbison, *Burgoyne and the Saratoga Campaign,* 336.
20. Burgoyne to Henry Laurens, 11 February 1778, Adams Matthew, Digital American Collection.
21. Details of the Convention agreement found in Fonblanque, *Political and Military Episodes,* 304–13; Cubbison, *Burgoyne and the Saratoga Campaign,* 321–41; Weddle, *Complete Victory,* 337–40; and Mintz, *Generals of Saratoga,* 220–23.
22. Cited in Cubbison, *Burgoyne and the Saratoga Campaign,* 340.
23. "Letters from Cambridge in New England," 15 November 1777, in *Letters from America 1776–1779,* trans. Ray W. Pettengill (Houghton Mifflin, 1924), 109.
24. Eliphalet Dyer to Horatio Gates, 5 November 1775, in *Letters of Delegates to Congress, 1774–1789,* ed. Paul H. Smith (Library of Congress, 1981), vol. 8, 233.
25. *Eighteenth-Century America: A Hessian Report on the People,* trans. Bruce E. Burgoyne (Heritage Books, 1995), 52.
26. John Andrews, *History of the War* (London, 1786), vol. 2, 414.
27. Gates's efforts to undermine Washington continued long after the victory of Saratoga. See Gerald W. Gawalt, *George Washington and Horatio Gates: The Man Who Would be King* (pub. by author, 2022); Mintz, *Generals at Saratoga,* 58–127; and Ron Chernow, *Washington: A Life* (Penguin, 2010), chap. 26.
28. John Rutledge to Henry Laurens, 7 November 1777, Adam Matthew, Digital Colonial America Collection.
29. Abigail Adams to John Adams, 22 October 1777, Adams Papers, MHS.
30. Samuel Cooper to John Adams, 22 October 1777, Adams Papers, MHS.

31. George Washington to Richard Henry Lee, 28 October 1777, in *Washington Papers: Revolutionary War Series* (University of Virginia Press, 2002), vol. 12, 41.
32. *Baroness Von Riedesel and the American Revolution,* ed. Marvin L. Brown Jr. (University of North Carolina Press, 1965), 55.
33. Cited in Fonblanque, *Political and Military Episodes,* 316–17.
34. See Frey, *The British Soldier in America;* Stephen Conway, *The British Army, 1714–1783: An Institutional History* (Pen and Sword Books, 2021); and Stephen Brumwell, *Redcoats: The British Soldier and War in the Americas 1755–1763* (Cambridge University Press, 2002).
35. Charles Stedman, *The History of the Origin, Progress, and Termination of the American War* (Dublin, 1794), vol. 2, 2.
36. "Letters from Cambridge," 15 November 1777, in *Letters from America 1776–1779,* trans. Ray W. Pettengill, 111.
37. Thomas Anburey, *Travels Through the Interior Parts of America* (London, 1789), vol. 2, 39.
38. Lamb, *Memoirs,* 373–74.
39. *Baroness Von Riedesel and the American Revolution,* 62.
40. William P. Upham, *A Memoir of General John Glover* (Salem, MA, 1863), 32; *Acts and Resolves,* vol. 20, 288–89.
41. Cited in Dorothy M. Vaughan, *"This Was a Man": A Biography of General William Whipple* (Stinehour Press, 1964), n.p. See also James Oliver Horton, *In Hope of Liberty: Culture, Community, and Protest Among Northern Free Blacks, 1700–1860* (Oxford University Press, 1997). Hannah Winthrop to Mercy Otis Warren, 11 November 1777, MHS.
42. *Letters of Brunswick and Hessian Officers During the American Revolution,* trans. William L. Stone (Albany, NY, 1891), 135–36.
43. *Memoirs and Letters and Journals of Major General Riedesel,* trans. William L. Stone (Albany, NY, 1868), 226.
44. *Letters from America 1776–1779,* trans. Ray W. Pettengill, 94.
45. *Letters of Brunswick and Hessian Officers,* 138.
46. *Letters of Brunswick and Hessian Officers,* 139.
47. *Letters of Brunswick and Hessian Officers,* 142–43.
48. *Letters of Brunswick and Hessian Officers,* 142–43.
49. Cited in Wikipedia, "Elizabeth Freeman."
50. Burgoyne, *State of the Expedition from Canada,* 45.
51. Thomas Anburey, *Travels Through the Interior Parts of America* (London, 1789), vol. 1, 29–30.

52. Anburey, *Travels,* vol. 1, 49–50.
53. Anburey, *Travels,* vol. 1, 31–33.
54. Samuel F. Batchelder, "Burgoyne and His Officers in Cambridge 1777–1778," *Proceedings,* Cambridge Historical Society, vol. 13, 26.
55. Hannah Winthrop to Mercy Otis Warren, 1 January 1774, MHS.
56. Hannah Winthrop to Mercy Otis Warren, 11 November 1777, MHS.
57. Hannah Winthrop to Mercy Otis Warren, 11 November 1777, MHS.
58. Hannah Winthrop to Mercy Otis Warren, 11 November 1777, MHS.
59. Hannah Winthrop to Mercy Otis Warren, 11 November 1777, MHS.
60. Cited in Batchelder, "Burgoyne and His Officers in Cambridge," 17.

4. LIVING WITH THE ENEMY

1. A detailed description of this remarkable dinner reception and stroll through central Boston as well as the quotations can be found in *Memoirs of Major-General William Heath,* ed. William Abbatt (New York, 1901) (originally published in Boston, 1798); hereafter cited as Heath, *Memoirs,* 125–27. Hannah Winthrop was among the spectators and informed her friend Mercy Otis Warren about the behavior of the American crowd (11 November 1777, Massachusetts Historical Society, Digital Collections; hereafter cited as MHS).
2. Nathaniel Hawthorne understood the symbolic significance of Province House. See "Legends of the Province-House" in *Twice-Told Tales* (Modern Library, 2001), 185; and "Province-House, in Boston, 1848," Historic New England website.
3. Heath, *Memoirs,* 127.
4. Heath to George Washington, 25 October 1777, Founders Online, National Archives; Heath to Jonathan Trumbull, 2 November 1777, MHS, Series 5, vol. 4 (1878), 172.
5. Winthrop to Warren, 11 November 1777, MHS.
6. Even at the time, the number of guards was a rough estimate (Heath to Washington, 25 October 1777, Founders Online).
7. "Regulations for the Troops of Lt. Genl. Burgoyne's Army," 8 November 1777, Adam Matthew, Digital Colonial America Collection; "From American Headquarters, Boston," 8 November 1777, in *Appendix to the Canada Papers, Relating Principally to the Convention Army After Its Arrival in the Neighbourhood of Boston* (Legare Street Press, 2018), ii–iv.

8. Samuel F. Batchelder, "Burgoyne and His Officers in Cambridge 1777–1778," *Proceedings,* Cambridge Historical Society, 14–66; Lucius R. Paige, *History of Cambridge, Massachusetts, 1630–1877* (Boston, 1877), 160.
9. Henry Hulton, *Henry Hulton and the American Revolution: An Outsider's Inside View,* ed. Neil Longley York (Colonial Society of Massachusetts, 2010), 270.
10. Thomas Anburey, *Travels Through the Interior Parts of America* (London, 1789), 67–70.
11. Winthrop to Warren, 11 November 1777, MHS; Paige, *History of Cambridge,* 160.
12. Oscar Handlin and Mary Handlin, eds., *The Popular Sources of Political Authority: Documents on the Massachusetts Constitution of 1780* (Harvard University Press, 1966), 1–54.
13. Handlin and Handlin, *The Popular Sources of Political Authority,* 231, 277, 278; *Continental Journal,* 9 April 1778.
14. T. H. Breen, *The Will of the People: The Revolutionary Birth of America* (Harvard University Press, 2019), chap. 5.
15. Cited in Breen, *The Will of the People,* 171, 174, 177; and Heath to Washington, 30 July 1777, Founders Online.
16. Cited in Samuel Batchelder, "Barracks on Cambridge Common, 1775–1918," *Harvard Graduates' Magazine* 28 (1919–20): 602; "The Revolutionary Journal of James Stevens of Andover, Mass.," *Essex Institute Collections* 48 (1912).
17. *Letters of Brunswick and Hessian Officers During the American Revolution,* trans. William L. Stone (Albany, NY, 1891), 15 November 1777, 156.
18. *Norwich (CT) Packet,* 10 November 1777.
19. Cited in Alexander J. Wall, "The Story of the Convention Army 1777–1783," *New York Historical Society Bulletin* 11 (1927): 77.
20. *Letters of Brunswick and Hessian Officers,* 153–54.
21. Anburey, *Travels,* 36.
22. *Memoirs and Letters and Journals of Major General Riedesel,* trans. William L. Stone (Albany, 1868), 224; Heath to Washington, 22 June 1778, Founders Online.
23. Washington to Heath, 23 May 1777, in *Washington Papers: Revolutionary War Series* (University of Viriginia Press, 1999), vol. 9, 503.
24. Anburey, *Travels,* 80–81.

25. *Journals of the House of Representatives of Massachusetts, 1776–1777* (Boston, 1986), vol. 53 (part 2), 227.
26. Burgoyne to Heath, 18 November 1777, in *Appendix to the Canada Papers,* xii; Burgoyne to Heath, 13 January 1778, in Adam Matthew, Digital Colonial America Collection; and *Letters from America 1776–1779,* trans. Ray W. Pettengill (Houghton Mifflin, 1924), 132–34.
27. James M. Hadden, *Hadden's Journal and Orderly Books* (Albany, NY 1884), 327; Mercy Otis Warren, *History of the Rise, Progress, and Termination of the American Revolution,* ed. Lester M. Cohen (Liberty Fund, 1989), vol. 2, 244.
28. *Continental Journal,* 19 December 1777.
29. Heath to Burgoyne, 28 January 1778, Adam Matthew, Digital Colonial America Collection.
30. *Acts and Resolves,* 9 January 1778, vol. 20, 229, 231.
31. *Boston Gazette,* 1 December 1777.
32. Heath to Washington, 25 October 1777, cited in Wall, "Story of the Convention Army," 71.
33. *Norwich (CT) Packet,* 10 November 1777.
34. Winthrop to Warren, 11 November 1777, MHS.
35. Winthrop to Warren, 4 February 1778, MHS.
36. *Independent Chronicle* (Boston), 26 February 1778. On the suffering of American prisoners, see Robert P. Watson, *The Ghost Ship of Brooklyn: An Untold Story of the American Revolution* (Da Capo, 2017).
37. Israel Evans, *A Discourse Delivered on the 18th Day of December 1777* (Boston, 1778), 20.
38. *Independent Chronicle* (Boston), 26 February 1778.
39. *Boston Gazette,* 6 November 1777.
40. Washington to Heath, 13 November 1777, Founders Online.
41. Footnote explaining Howe's secret letter to Burgoyne following Washington to Heath, 13 November 1777, Founders Online. See Jane Clark, "Responsibility for the Failure of the Burgoyne Campaign," *American Historical Review* 35 (1930): 542–59.
42. Washington to Heath, 22 January 1778, Founders Online.
43. *Boston Gazette,* 16 February 1778.
44. Heath, *Memoirs,* 135.
45. Heath, *Memoirs,* 130–33.
46. The fullest treatment of the Cambridge housing crisis is Batchelder, "Burgoyne and His Officers," 14–68.

47. Cited in Batchelder, "Burgoyne and His Officers," 26.
48. Batchelder, "Burgoyne and His Officers," 38.
49. Batchelder, "Burgoyne and His Officers," 31.
50. Burgoyne to Heath, 10 November 1777, in *Appendix to the Canada Papers,* v.
51. Heath to Burgoyne, 11 November 1777, in *Appendix to the Canada Papers,* vi.
52. *Memoirs of Major General Riedesel,* 220.
53. William Gordon, *History of the Rise, Progress, and Establishment of the Independence of the United States of America* (New York, 1788), vol. 2, 298.

5. BREACH OF PUBLIC FAITH

1. On the many challenges facing the new national government, see Jack N. Rakove, *The Beginnings of National Politics: An Interpretive History of the Continental Congress* (Johns Hopkins University Press, 1979); and Edmund Cody Burnett, *The Continental Congress from Its Inception in 1774 to March 1789* (Norton, 1964).
2. George R. Prowell, *Continental Congress at York, Pennsylvania and York County in the Revolution* (York Printing Co., 1914), 289–300.
3. Cited in John Brewer, *The Sinews of Power: War, Money and the English States, 1688–1783* (Harvard University Press, 1990), 187.
4. *The Adams Papers: Diary and Autobiography,* ed. L. H. Butterfield (Atheneum, 1964), vol. 2, 173.
5. Eliphalet Dyer to Jonathan Trumbull, 5 January 1778, in *Letters of Delegates to Congress,* ed. Paul H. Smith (Library of Congress, 1981), vol. 8, 527–29.
6. *The Papers of Henry Laurens, 1 November 1777–15 March 1778* (University of South Carolina Press, 1990), vol. 12; S. Max Edelson, *Plantation Enterprise in Colonial South Carolina* (Harvard University Press, 2006), chap. 6.
7. Laurens to Heath, *Letters of Delegates,* 244, 485–86.
8. Laurens to Heath, 27 December 1777, *Letters of Delegates,* 485–86.
9. Laurens to Heath, 27 December 1777, *Letters of Delegates,* 485–86; *Memoirs of Major-General William Heath,* ed. William Abbatt (New York, 1901) (originally published in Boston, 1798), 134; hereafter cited as Heath, *Memoirs;* Norman S. Poser, *From the Battlefield to the Stage: The Many Lives of General John Burgoyne* (McGill-Queen's University Press, 2022), 151–52.

10. *Journals of the Continental Congress 1774–1789,* ed. Worthington Chauncey Ford (Government Printing Office, 1908), vol. 10, 29.
11. *Boston Gazette,* 16 February 1778.
12. *Boston Gazette,* 16 February 1778.
13. *Journals of the Continental Congress,* vol. 10, 31.
14. *Journals of the Continental Congress,* vol. 10, 15–16; Dyer to Trumbull, 5 January 1778, in *Letters of the Delegates,* 527.
15. *Journals of the Continental Congress,* vol. 10, 13.
16. *Journals of the Continental Congress,* vol. 10, 6; Laurens to Heath, 27 December 1777, in *Letters of the Delegates,* 486; *Boston Gazette,* 16 February 1778.
17. Henry Laurens to John Laurens, 14 January 1778, in *Letters of the Delegates,* 592.
18. Gideon Mailer, *John Witherspoon's American Revolution* (University of North Carolina Press, 2017); John Witherspoon, *The Works of John Witherspoon* (Edinburgh, 1804), vol. 9, 73.
19. "John Witherspoon's Speech in Congress," 8 January 1778, in *Letters of the Delegates,* 551.
20. "John Witherspoon's Speech in Congress," 8 January 1778, in *Letters of the Delegates,* 553–54.
21. "John Witherspoon's Speech in Congress," 8 January 1778, in *Letters of the Delegates,* 554.
22. "John Witherspoon's Speech in Congress," 8 January 1778, in *Letters of the Delegates,* 554.
23. "John Witherspoon's Speech in Congress," 8 January 1778, in *Letters of the Delegates,* 555.
24. "John Witherspoon's Speech in Congress," 8 January 1778, in *Letters of the Delegates,* 555–56.
25. Henry Laurens to George Clinton, 14 January 1778, in *Letters of the Delegates,* 588.
26. Laurens to Marquis de Lafayette, 12 January 1778, in *Letters of the Delegates,* 572–73.
27. Laurens to Baron de Kalb, 22 January 1778, in *Letters of the Delegates,* 34.
28. Henry Laurens to John Laurens, 14 January 1778, in *Letters of the Delegates,* 592.
29. "Henry Laurens's Notes," (1782?), in *Letters of the Delegates,* 542–44.
30. "Henry Laurens's Notes," (1782?), in *Letters of the Delegates,* 543. What it meant to be a trustworthy nation remained a major concern for

American political leaders long after the end of the Revolution. See Eliga H. Gould, *Among the Powers of the Earth: The American Revolution and the Making of a New World Empire* (Harvard University Press, 2012).

6. AMERICAN AT THE BAR

1. *Letters of Brunswick and Hessian Officers During the American Revolution,* trans. William L. Stone (Albany, NY, 1891), 161, 163.
2. *Letters of Brunswick and Hessian Officers,* 135–36.
3. George Washington to Jeremiah Dummer Powell, 28 May 1777, in *Washington Papers: Revolutionary War Series* (University of Virginia Press, 1999), vol. 9, 550.
4. William Tudor to John Adams, 29 September 1776, Founders Online, National Archives.
5. *Memoirs of Major-General William Heath,* ed. William Abbatt (New York, 1901) (originally published in Boston, 1798), 138; hereafter cited as Heath, *Memoirs.*
6. "General Orders," 24 September 1776, Founders Online; Heath, *Memoirs,* 56–57; Tudor to John Adams, 23 September 1776, Founders Online.
7. Mercy Otis Warren, *History of the Rise, Progress, and Termination of the American Revolution,* ed. Lester M. Cohen (Liberty Fund, 1989), vol. 2, 244.
8. *Proceedings of a General Court-Martial Held at Cambridge* (Boston, 1778), 5.
9. Heath, *Memoirs,* 138–39.
10. Heath to Burgoyne, 9 January 1778, *Appendix to the Canada Papers,* xxxi–xxxii; Heath to Burgoyne, 9 January 1778, Adam Matthew, Digital Colonial America Collection.
11. Heath, *Memoirs,* 140.
12. Heath, *Memoirs,* 141.
13. Burgoyne to Heath, 13 January 1778, in *Appendix to the Canada Papers,* xxxvi.
14. Heath to Burgoyne, 15 January 1778, in *Appendix to the Canada Papers,* xlii.
15. Heath to Burgoyne, 15 January 1778, in *Appendix to the Canada Papers,* xlii.
16. Burgoyne to Heath, 12 January 1778, Adam Matthew, Digital Colonial America Collection.
17. Burgoyne to Heath, 12 January 1778, Adam Matthew, Digital Colonial America Collection.

18. "Answers to Burgoyne's Questions," 14 January 1778, Adam Matthew, Digital Colonial America Collection.
19. Stephen Payne Adye, *A Treatise on Courts Martial* (New York, 1769), 28.
20. Heath to Burgoyne, 13 January 1778, Adam Matthew, Digital Colonial America Collection.
21. Heath to Burgoyne, 13 January 1778, Adam Matthew, Digital Colonial America Collection.
22. *Substance of General Burgoyne's Speeches at a Court-Martial Held at Cambridge* (Newport, RI, 1778), 4.
23. Heath to Washington, 19 January 1778, Founders Online.
24. Adye, *A Treatise,* iii.
25. Adye, *A Treatise,* 107.
26. George Washington to John Hancock, 24 July 1776, University of Michigan Library, Digital Collection.
27. *Rules and Regulations for the Massachusetts Army* (Salem, MA, 1775), 3.
28. *Rules and Regulations for the Massachusetts Army,* 3.
29. "Articles of War," 20 September 1776, Avalon Project (Yale University), Documents in Law, History and Diplomacy (online); John Adams to James Warren, 25 September 1776, Founders Online.
30. "Articles of War," Article 47.
31. William Winthrop, *Military Law and Precedents* (Government Printing Office, 1920), 711. See also Joshua Kastenberg, *The Blackstone of Military Law: Colonel William Winthrop* (Scarecrow, 2009).
32. Winthrop, *Military Law,* 710–11.

7. ENEMY FOR THE PROSECUTION

1. *Substance of General Burgoyne's Speeches at a Court-Martial Held at Cambridge* (Newport, RI, 1778), 18.
2. The announcement appeared in *Boston Gazette,* 1 June 1778; *Independent Chronicle,* 28 May 1778; and *Continental Journal,* 6 August 1778. The full title of the Boston publication is *The Proceedings of a General Court-Martial Held at Cambridge, On Tuesday the Twentieth of January; and Continued by Several Adjournments to Wednesday the 25th of February, 1778: Upon the Trial of Colonel David Henley;* hereafter cited as *Proceedings,* Boston.
3. *Boston Gazette,* 1 June 1778.
4. *Letters of Brunswick and Hessian Officers During the American Revolution,* trans. William L. Stone (Albany, NY, 1891), 168.

5. The full title of the London publication is *Proceedings of a Court-Martial Held at Cambridge by Order of Major General Heath, Commanding the American Troops for the Northern District, for the Trial of Colonel David Henley, Accused by General Burgoyne of Ill Treatment of the British Soldiers* (London, 1778); hereafter cited as *Proceedings*, London. See *Encyclopedia Britannica 1911,* under "John Almon," online.
6. *Dictionary of Canadian Biography,* vol. 6 (1821–1835), under "John Howe," online.
7. *Letters of Brunswick and Hessian Officers,* 161–62.
8. Heath to Washington, 27 November 1777, Founders Online, National Archives.
9. Washington to Heath, 17 December 1777, Founders Online.
10. "William Tudor," *Sibley's Harvard Graduates* (Boston, 1975), vol. 42, 252–65.
11. Cited in "William Tudor," *Sibley's Harvard Graduates* (Boston, 1975), vol. 42, 253.
12. Cited in Francis Josiah Hudleston, *Gentleman Johnny Burgoyne: Misadventures of an English General in the Revolution* (Bobbs-Merrill, 1927), 275.
13. Stephen Payne Adye, *A Treatise on Courts Martial* (New York, 1769), 35.
14. Adye, *A Treatise,* 36–37.
15. *Proceedings,* Boston, 73.
16. *Proceedings,* Boston, 8.
17. *Proceedings,* Boston, 71.
18. *Proceedings,* Boston, 73–74.
19. *Proceedings,* Boston, 73–74.
20. *Substance of General Burgoyne's Speeches,* 5–6.
21. *Proceedings,* Boston, 74.
22. *Proceedings,* Boston, 74.
23. *Proceedings,* Boston, 74.
24. *Substance of General Burgoyne's Speeches,* 5–6.
25. *Substance of General Burgoyne's Speeches,* 3.
26. *Substance of General Burgoyne's Speeches,* 4.
27. *Substance of General Burgoyne's Speeches,* 3.
28. *Substance of General Burgoyne's Speeches,* 3–4.
29. *Letters from America 1776–1779,* trans. Ray W. Pettengill (Boston, 1924), 137.
30. *Substance of General Burgoyne's Speeches,* 5.
31. *Substance of General Burgoyne's Speeches,* 5.

32. *Proceedings,* Boston, 9.
33. *Proceedings,* Boston, 12; *Proceedings,* London, 15.
34. *Proceedings,* London, 17.
35. *Proceedings,* Boston, 14.
36. *Proceedings,* London, 31; *Proceedings,* Boston, 19–20.
37. *Proceedings,* London, 21; *Proceedings,* Boston, 14–15.
38. *Proceedings,* London, 21–22; *Proceedings,* Boston, 14–15.
39. *Proceedings,* London, 24; *Proceedings,* Boston, 16.
40. *Proceedings,* London, 22; *Proceedings,* Boston, 15.
41. *Proceedings,* London, 28; *Proceedings,* Boston, 18.
42. *Proceedings,* London, 54; *Proceedings,* Boston, 31–32.
43. *Proceedings,* London, 57; *Proceedings,* Boston, 33.
44. *Proceedings,* London, 58; *Proceedings,* Boston, 34.
45. *Proceedings,* London, 62; *Proceedings,* Boston, 36.
46. *Proceedings, London,* 58; *Proceedings,* Boston, 7.
47. *Proceedings,* London, 65; *Proceedings,* Boston, 15.
48. *Proceedings,* London, 66; *Proceedings,* Boston, 38.
49. *Proceedings,* London, 67; *Proceedings,* Boston, 16.
50. *Proceedings,* London, 68; *Proceedings,* Boston, 17.
51. *Proceedings,* London, 71; *Proceedings,* Boston, 18.

8. FOR THE DEFENSE

1. *The Proceedings of a General Court-Martial Held at Cambridge, On Tuesday the Twentieth of January; and Continued by Several Adjournments to Wednesday the 25th of February, 1778: Upon the Trial of Colonel David Henley,* 41; hereafter cited as *Proceedings,* Boston.
2. *Proceedings,* Boston, 42–43.
3. *Proceedings,* Boston, 46.
4. *Proceedings,* Boston, 48.
5. *Proceedings,* Boston, 50.
6. *Proceedings,* Boston, 51.
7. *Proceedings,* Boston, 54.
8. *Proceedings,* Boston, 54.
9. *Proceedings,* Boston, 55, 57–58.
10. *Proceedings,* Boston, 65–66.
11. *Proceedings,* Boston, 69–70.
12. *Proceedings,* Boston, 70.

13. *Proceedings*, Boston, 71.
14. *Proceedings*, Boston, 74.
15. *Substance of General Burgoyne's Speeches at a Court-Martial Held at Cambridge* (Newport, RI, 1778), 6.
16. *Proceedings of a Court-Martial Held at Cambridge by Order of Major General Heath, Commanding the American Troops for the Northern District, for the Trial of Colonel David Henley, Accused by General Burgoyne of Ill Treatment of the British Soldiers* (London, 1778), 122–23; hereafter cited as *Proceedings*, London.
17. *Proceedings*, London, 122–23.
18. *Proceedings*, London, 124.
19. *Proceedings*, London, 131–33.
20. *Proceedings*, London, 133.
21. *Proceedings*, London, 135.
22. *Proceedings*, London, 137.
23. *Proceedings*, London, 137.
24. *Proceedings*, London, 138–39.
25. *Proceedings*, Boston, 75.
26. *Proceedings*, Boston, 76.
27. *Proceedings*, Boston, 76.
28. *Proceedings*, Boston, 76.
29. *Proceedings*, Boston, 79.
30. *Proceedings*, Boston, 79.
31. *Proceedings*, Boston, 79.
32. *Proceedings*, Boston, 79–80.
33. *Proceedings*, Boston, 81.
34. *Proceedings*, Boston, 81.
35. *Proceedings*, London, 143; *Proceedings*, Boston, 81. See Kevin Weddle, *The Complete Victory: Saratoga and the American Revolution* (Oxford University Press, 2021), 174–77.
36. *Proceedings*, Boston, 83.
37. *Proceedings*, Boston, 86.
38. *Proceedings*, Boston, 87.
39. *Proceedings*, Boston, 88.
40. *Independent Chronicle*, 12 March 1778.
41. Winthrop to Warren, 4 February 1778, Massachusetts Historical Society, Digital Collections; hereafter cited as MHS.
42. *Boston Gazette*, 9 February 1778.

43. *Massachusetts Spy,* 5 February 1778.
44. *Continental Journal,* 7 January 1778.
45. *Continental Journal,* 7 January 1778. The story of the aristocratic exchange of prisoners was still circulating a decade later (*Massachusetts Gazette,* 4 November 1788).
46. *Boston Gazette,* 9 February 1778.
47. *Boston Gazette,* 9 February 1778.
48. *New-Jersey Gazette,* 25 February 1778.
49. *Independent Chronicle,* 26 February 1778.
50. *Memoirs of Major-General William Heath,* ed. William Abbatt (New York, 1901) (originally published in Boston, 1798), 143.

EPILOGUE

1. T. Cole Jones, *Captives of Liberty: Prisoners of War and the Politics of Vengeance in the American Revolution* (University of Pennsylvania Press, 2020).
2. *Memoirs of Major-General William Heath,* ed. William Abbatt (New York, 1901) (originally published in Boston, 1798), 148; hereafter cited as Heath, *Memoirs.*
3. Marquis De Chastellux, *Travels in North America* (University of North Carolina Press, 1963), 48.
4. David Henley to Robert Kingston, 30 March 1778, Gilder Lehrman Institute of American History, GLC 04764,68. As an intelligence officer, Washington to Henley, 18 November 1778, in *Washington Papers: Revolutionary War Series* (University of Virginia Press, 2008), vol. 18, 195–296.
5. *The French Broad–Holston Country: A History of Knox County, Tennessee,* ed. Mary U. Rothrock (East Tennessee Historical Society, 1946), 426–28.
6. Francis S. Drake, *The Town of Roxbury; Its Memorable Persons and Places* (Boston Municipal Printing Office, 1905), 387.
7. Peleg W. Chandler, *American Criminal Trials* (Boston, 1844), vol. 2, 152.

• INDEX •

Italicized page numbers refer to illustrations.

ALSO BY T. H. BREEN

American Insurgents, American Patriots: The Revolution of the People

The Marketplace of Revolution: How Consumer Politics Shaped American Independence

Tobacco Culture: The Mentality of the Great Tidewater Planters on the Eve of Revolution

The Will of the People: The Revolutionary Birth of America

THE REVOLUTIONARY AGE

The American Revolution at 250: Twenty-Four Historians Reflect on the Founding
Francis D. Cogliano, editor

The Global Age of Revolutions: A History from 1650 to Today
Bryan A. Banks and Cindy Ermus, editors

Barbary Entanglements: Realizing American Independence on the World Stage
John M. Chamberlin

The Course of Human Events: The Declaration of Independence and the Historical Origins of the United States
Steven Sarson

Napoleon in America: Bonaparte and the Rhetoric of US Empire
Mark F. Ehlers

Before Manifest Destiny: The Contested Expansion of the Early United States
Nicholas G. DiPucchio

Revolutionary Diplomacy: Spanish Connections and the Birth of the United States
Thomas E. Chávez

Declarations of Independence: Indigenous Resilience, Colonial Rivalries, and the Cost of Revolution
Christopher R. Pearl

Dishonored Americans: The Political Death of Loyalists in Revolutionary America
Timothy Compeau

The American Liberty Pole: Popular Politics and the Struggle for Democracy in the Early Republic
Shira Lurie

European Friends of the American Revolution
Andrew J. O'Shaughnessy, John A. Ragosta, and Marie-Jeanne Rossignol, editors

The Tory's Wife: A Woman and Her Family in Revolutionary America
Cynthia A. Kierner

Writing Early America: From Empire to Revolution
Trevor Burnard

Spain and the American Revolution: New Approaches and Perspectives
Gabriel Paquette and Gonzalo M. Quintero Saravia, editors

The American Revolution and the Habsburg Monarchy
Jonathan Singerton

Navigating Neutrality: Early American Governance in the Turbulent Atlantic
Sandra Moats

Ireland and America: Empire, Revolution, and Sovereignty
Patrick Griffin and Francis D. Coogliano, editors